How To

INCREASE PRODUCTIVITY

By Working

LESS Hours

ISBN-13:

978-1489560896

ISBN-10:

1489560890

ABOUT THE AUTHOR

About the Author

Shaun McDonogh is an experienced Finance Director, Financial Planning & Analysis (FP&A) Manager, Trainer and Microsoft Excel wizard. During his career, Shaun has reaped tremendous benefits from applying a unique combination of Lean based principles in reporting, along with unseen techniques to achieve unthinkable results in his work environment (through increased productivity) and family life (through working less hours).

Qualifications include not only Shaun's academics, but also his certificate in 'Lean Leadership Facilitation', which he received at the age of 25 from the Minnesota School of Engineering (MSOE), offered as an opportunity through his employment at a Fortune 500 Manufacturing and Engineering giant.

Author's Note

The knowledge and techniques I will be sharing with you in this book have transformed my life. I sincerely wish you the very best in your career, and am confident that you will gain much strength in your day to day work approach from reading through these simple yet highly effective techniques. Good luck in your endeavours to becoming highly effective in your environment!

CONTENTS

Preface: About this Book 1

PART I: LEAN MEETS INFORMATION FLOW 2

Introduction to Lean 3
  "Adrenaline Junkies" 3
  What is Lean? 5
  Is Financial Modelling ("FM") Part Of Lean? 7

1 - A New Case for Lean: Reporting 9
  Product Flow versus Information Flow 9
  Process, Process, Process and MPTR © 13

2 - Defining Value, Seeking Perfection............................17
  Efficiency 17
  Productivity and the 5 Principles of Lean.....................21

3 - Spreadsheet Samurai 27
  Become Lazy 27
  Financial Modelling – Purpose 28
  Financial Modelling – Function 30

PART II: OUT WITH THE OLD, IN WITH THE NEW
.... 37

4 – Cleaning Out Your Closet with '5S' 38
  Sort..39
  Set-in-Order 42
  Shine 44
  Standardise 45

Sustain..45

5 - Value Stream Mapping: A Powerful Tool 47
What is Value Stream Mapping (VSM)?.......................48
Define and Document a Business Case 51
Assemble a Lean Team / Delegate Tasks 52
Identify Scope, Identify Value, Know Your Customer 53
Organise the Meeting 56
Calculate TAKT Time..56
Start the Exercise! 57
Highlight Value, Bottlenecks and Rework 58
Document Process Time and Waiting Time 59
Document Suggestions on Effort-Benefit Matrix 60
Repeat for Future State and Follow Up.......................61

6 - Starting with Mindset 64
Attitude 65
You and Your Organisation 66
Managing Upwards 67
Define Success, Set Goals...69
Manage Email...70
Final Word on Mindset 71

**PART III: AUTOMATION: FINANCIAL MODELLING
MADE USEFUL 72**

7 - Automation: Data Becomes Information 73
Data Structure..77

8 - Toolbox: Spreadsheet Functions and Techniques 80
Functions – SUM 81
Functions – SUMIF Technique.....................................82
PivotTable, a SUMIF Replication 89
Functions – VLOOKUP on the Stock Market.................94
Functions – IF You Could IF 98

A Note on Presentation..102

9 - Creativity Evokes Change **103**
Creativity...103
Final Word...104

GLOSSARY **106**

BIBLIOGRAPHY **109**

NOTES **111**

Preface: About this Book

If your management told you to be TWICE as effective, would you work TWICE the hours?! Of course not. It's impossible. The solution isn't to work MORE hours, but to work LESS! Quite apart from the obvious health risks mentioned in Forbes' "Why Working More Than 8 Hours A Day Can Kill You," to be truly efficient we need to change our culture, by learning to achieve better results WITHOUT the 'easy' solution of working more hours.

We all know the saying, "Work smarter, not harder, but do we know how to put it into practice? YES! You achieve results by making the eight hour working day work for you!" In this book you will be shown a unique technique that Finance Director and Author, Shaun McDonogh, has developed through his years of experience and training. Shaun shows you how to achieve greater productivity by using the 8 hour working day to your advantage.

Shaun demonstrates that the secret formula of success is to apply the Japanese 'Lean' philosophy to eliminate waste. By improving your processes and using a few simple tools and techniques available to us all, you can achieve unthinkable results...

PART I: Lean Meets Information Flow

Introduction to Lean

"The most dangerous kind of waste is the waste we do not recognize."

~ Shigeo Shingo

"Adrenaline Junkies"

We fed ourselves on stress, anxiety and adrenaline. Back then, finance office workers in this FTSE publishing company would work until two in the morning on a regular basis. We considered ourselves friends, soldiers battling a never ending battery of month-end deadlines.

I remember a good friend and colleague of mine being hospitalised due to work related stress. We would talk amongst ourselves about the senior management, who didn't seem at all concerned. There appeared to be a 'glass ceiling,' and if anyone did ever get promoted it just meant twice the work and twice the hours with almost no additional pay.

The work experience was excellent if you were willing to take the opportunities presented. However, most of us analysts, bookkeepers and accountants at the time were apprehensive about adding anything more to what was the already over-piled workload. I was 21 years of age at the time. I was hungry for experience, a promotion and additional pay.

My relationship with my son suffered due to a lack of physical and mental energy on my part. The long hours and commute to work day in and day out seemed to drain me completely of the substance required to sustain friendships and spend time with family. My finances were at an all-time low. I had barely any relationship with friends, and the work pressure was mounting, fast!

Fed up with working so hard for such little reward, I made a decision which would change my career and life forever. From applying the principles in this book, not only would I turn the most enlightening corner of my working career, but I would have fun doing it too!

I made a personal decision to leave at 5:00 pm every working day with zero working hours at weekends. This was not announced to anyone. I figured if I lost my job, at least I would have more time with family. However, there was no giving up without a fight. The challenge was not only to leave at the contracted time, but also to meet the management's expectations.

Three months later I was promoted. My personal life had flourished, and not only did I hit targets and deadlines, but I was helping others too with the time I had to spare. I had learned that not only were my previous ideas and thoughts about the management and company wrong, they were also made self-fulfilling by my previous beliefs. As the old saying goes,

"If you want things to change, YOU have to change!"

Now seven years later, I work as a Finance Director for a large multimillion dollar business, trying to cram as much value as I can into my working life by banishing waste from my task list. What's more, I enjoy my work, and enjoy helping others, as well as having the time I need to support my family. I am not looking to boast. There are many things I have failed at and could have done much better. I am still a lifetime away from perfection in what I do. I am simply stating that if my mindset had not changed, I would still be on 25% of my current salary, working twice the hours. That is the impact of thinking 'LEAN *(9)*' by employing Lean principles into your daily routine.

So how was it possible to could go from being a person swamped in administrative work and drowning in endless deadlines, to someone who achieved twice the output in half the time?

The answer comes from a change in your mindset, implementation of a new management process *(10)* and sharpening your automation skills (in my case using financial modelling) to achieve results far beyond what most accountants could have dreamt possible. The answer more simply put, is applying Lean principles into your everyday administrative tasks. We need to work fewer hours in order to achieve productivity through smart processes, not the other way around!

What is Lean?

It was two years earlier when my jaw almost hit the floor. I heard an employee saying to our CFO at the multi-billion dollar fortune 500 company,

"We do not want to make our jobs more efficient because then we will be fired, we are working ourselves out of a job if we do as you ask!"

Before telling you what your instincts already know about what Lean is, let me tell you first about what lean isn't.

Lean is NOT a strategy for cutting headcount. Lean is a growth strategy. It is designed for us to create more efficient processes so that we can increase time spent on value adding tasks and reduce time spent on non-value adding tasks. More value means making the cash bag bigger and providing an avenue for organic growth. Therefore helping the organisation to grow and support our jobs and salaries.

Lean is NOT only applicable to manufacturing. You will note from the previous example that there is a significant amount of waste in the administrative environment (Finance in particular).

Lean is NOT an excuse to spend capital on fixing issues. Yes, there are times when this is necessary. However, Lean seeks to eliminate waste. Often our 'spend more money' solutions are just like another process 'bandage'.

Human nature has a tendency to only treat the symptoms, without truly resolving the causes of an problem. This is why people work additional hours. Our laziness when it comes to looking at the root causes of problems, and to find effective solutions, has brought about a working culture which I do not subscribe to. I am referring to the type of culture whereby if we work late we are perceived to be working hard and therefore 'earning our bread'. Avoid this culture! It will keep you in a prison of long hours, wearing you down and making you ineffective.

Lean is NOT is not rocket science. It is easy to figure out. Lean is about having outstanding processes which can be managed by average people rather than having expensive people managing average processes. This was the belief of Toyota when it took the world by storm by implementing Lean principles, growing their business 8 fold.

Lean is NOT a destination, but rather a journey of continuous improvement. This is referred to in Japanese as 'Kaizen'.

Alright, I think you get the point.... Lean in principle is about identifying value and eliminating waste. As Shigeo Shingo, renowned Japanese engineer and creator of the 'Lean' philosophy said, "The most dangerous kind of waste is the waste we do not recognize." Can you imagine how much unrecognisable waste exists in finance and administration?!

We will discuss this in much more depth in the first part of this book.

Is Financial Modelling ("FM") Part Of Lean?

If it contains identifiable value and helps eliminate waste, then yes, absolutely! Financial Modelling ('FM') is important for standardisation or streamlining within an information flow [4] environment. However, having strong skills with spreadsheets is also far underrated, particularly within the finance community. If you were a surgeon would you want to work with a scalpel which is blunt? No! Of course not, and your patients wouldn't want you to either. If you were a carpenter who cut wood with a spoon rather than a saw (ok, an extreme example I know), wouldn't you expect to work 10 times your normal hours, to achieve the same results?

Having strong spreadsheet skills is the same in principle. I know it has helped me tremendously. You first need to sharpen your tools, before being confident about streamlining your work processes. This does not only relate to spreadsheets, but to whichever system you use most. Invest the time to become an expert with your chosen tools. Be the person others come to if they have a 'how-to' question.

I learned to use Microsoft Excel using the "For Dummies" guides. You don't need to be highly advanced to be highly efficient. You just need to grasp all the fundamentals to keep your tool box in check.

However, financial modelling is only the tool. You will also need to learn more about the right mindset, processes and results orientated goal setting. These are all discussed in the coming chapters.

1 - A New Case for Lean: Reporting

"You cannot solve today's problems with today's thinking".

~ Albert Einstein

Product Flow versus Information Flow

"Why" is probably the most useful word in your vocabulary when it comes to driving change in your daily processes.

Questioning "why" something is the case, or "why can't we do it another way?" or "why do we have this meeting?" is one of the most provocative approaches, and the most productive, rattling the bars of our own self-imposed process prisons.

"Why are we not focussing on Lean within the finance or admin environment? I am sure there is plenty of waste there?" was asked in front of various highly qualified business production and manufacturing leaders on a three week intensive Lean training course.

The simple answer provided was,

"It is… you can '5S' *(16)* your office space and label all your stationery."

The highly intelligent and well-educated Lean training professional who said this was not joking. This was at the time the focus was on Lean based administration, and his answer did not satisfy my curiosity in the slightest. Lean principles were very much associated with production, engineering and manufacturing on this particular course. In other words, Lean was having an extremely beneficial impact associated with Product flow.

However, one has to ask the question, how much waste is associated with Information flow? Let us compare waste between the two.

The website isixsigma.com tells us there are 8 traditional product related wastes of Lean:

1) Transport: Moving people, products & information

2) Inventory: Storing parts, pieces, documentation ahead of requirements

3) Motion: Bending, turning, reaching, lifting

4) Waiting : For parts, information, instructions, equipment

5) Over production: Making more than is immediately required

6) Over processing: Tighter tolerances or higher grade materials than are necessary

7) Defects: Rework, scrap, incorrect documentation

8) Skills: Underutilizing capabilities, delegating tasks with inadequate training

Let us now apply some examples of information related waste to the above:

1) Transport: Moving information from a source document to reporting. Sources may include delivery notes, invoices, schedules, sales performance metrics etc., which can be entered into a reporting system. Think about it another way; does information appear in a system from nowhere? Of course not. There is a cost to carrying and reconciling information. That cost is usually people related.

2) Inventory: Data storage. This is fairly discrete when comparing within a finance or administration function. However, consider what a company like Google might spend on storing their data which has billions of entries every day. Storage can very quickly become a significant issue and should not be overlooked. There is a cost to holding the information you save.

3) Motion/over processing/defects: These three items can be grouped together and put as 'GIGO', 'Garbage In Garbage Out'. Information starts with data. Useful information starts with useful data.

A team I worked with previously quantified the amount of people hours spent in a particular finance reporting process known as 'Flash'. We calculated that around 2,000 human hours were wasted reworking data. If you apply this to an average salary the cost to the business was around $30,000 each time this process was performed. This occurred monthly. The reason behind the wasteful reworking was due to regional results being refined over and over again before reporting the reworked data to the next management level (for more reworking) and so on.

Working at the top of the reporting chain for this particular process, our team was very quickly able to determine the value of this information. Very often it was not credible and thus carried zero value. Had we extracted the financials another way without requiring the rework by each reporting level, the organisation could have saved around $360,000 per year.

4) Waiting: How often do you have to start compiling an ad-hoc report which should have been prepared for you, just because someone was late delivering the information you needed? Then the report turns up late, and is nothing like you expected? Information should be instant - given that the data exists. How long does it take for you to receive information when it is available in a system? Milliseconds? Ok, a report may have to be run - but could that not be automated to run when you are out the office?

5) Over production: In my experience this is the worst type of waste. We are to blame just as much as our managers. We need to be better at defining WHAT we need, and then deliver this message. Everyone seems to think that they must have all possible information available all the time, regardless of its value. As though this makes us appear to be on top of our daily challenges, that we can show we know everything that we could possibly be asked.

This approach is dangerous. I believe we need to change our attitude here. We only need information which is useful and of value. Value will determine the effectiveness of our decision making. True analysis *(2)* involves having information which supports taking corrective action. If the information does not help us add value in the business, then why do we need it?

How much time is wrapped up in the reporting element of your job? Remember to manage upwards. We will discuss this in more detail later.

6) Skills: Choose automation, for example. How much of your time do you spend using systems like Microsoft Office,

SAP, Excel etc.? These systems should be treated as if they are your staff. They work for you. At least they do if you tell them to. The sharper your skills the more efficient you are, because the more you can delegate to the systems you use.

The 6th point above was one of the turning points in turning my career around. It helped me automate tasks which most people believed required a human to perform. The reality, whether we want to admit it or not, is that if a process involves 100% logic it can be 100% automated. If you figure the logic you are using then you can then ask someone (if you don't know yourself) to program that logic into your system. If there were only five important aspects of this book you want to write down, then make this one of them!

Product is not where the principles of Lean end. You can employ Lean principles into your scope of control. Change the flow of information by using techniques taught in this book and you will be sure to see results right away.

Process, Process, Process and MPTR ©

"A bad system will beat a good person every time."

~W. Edwards Deming

Have you ever sat in a meeting where you felt out of your depth? If so, you will know the daunting feeling of being under enormous pressure to reach a new level of conscious attention, at least until the meeting ends. Everything can seem very complex when you are not familiar with the people, process or meeting aim. A man shouted out to the company regional President "we need to double our throughput *(14)* year on year if you want us to achieve that target." I whispered very timidly and cautiously to our CFO (Chief Financial Officer), "How will we do that?" to which he replied,

"PROCESS!, PROCESS!, PROCESS!, It's all about PROCESS!"

That realisation changed me. Things were never the same again. For some reason everything became less confusing. I realised that the reason we were going to achieve greatness in our organisation was not because all the people in the room were complete genius master minds, contrary to my previous thinking. No, we were going to achieve our goals through managing processes which average people including myself could understand. Therefore, if I could understand the underlying process, I could be involved in the discussions too. Better yet, if you can understand a process which needs improving (or removing) then you can make a difference.

Would you have ideas and not be afraid to ask "why"? We do this naturally all the time. If you can tap into this understanding it will not only have a tremendous impact on your own work (and even home) environment, but from experience I believe you will also be able to help others too. Any by helping others you will build key relationships and be more fulfilled when working the 9-5 regime.

Process cannot be the only focus. We need to be cognisant of the bigger picture. You need to have the right mindset, one which uses tools to achieve the desired results. The MPTR © model is a summary of this:

Figure 1.1 – MPTR C

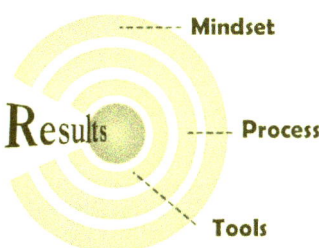

This model has been designed to help you understand the four main components that will help you to achieve greater efficiency in your working life.

Mindset: The first and most important of the four rings is the mindset. You will need to be well equipped mentally to approach your challenges, colleagues and challenging colleagues on problem solving discussions. You will also need a 'can-do' attitude with a willingness to believe there is almost always a more efficient way, given that waste is ever present. This is the first area, and it encompasses all other principles.

Process: As prescribed by the CFO, an essential step towards achieving greater efficiency is to have strong processes which average people can follow.

However, at times the best process is having no process at all - by removing unnecessary tasks. Sometimes you may be able to remove an entire process altogether. This is a great feeling, which can also help motivate both yourself and your team alike.

Tools: We mentioned about being exceptional at using relevant IT systems. However, learning commonly used systems like spreadsheets and being proficient using email are not the only ways to utilise tools available. Sometimes we can create tools which act as visual "Kanban" *(7)* signals. These will help us to run processes and make decisions more quickly and efficiently than without having any tools at all.

Results: Ok I admit it. I said that mindset was the most important. However, you cannot have great processes with great tools and have the best attitude when the results do not count. We do all this because we want results. It is likely that you are reading this to learn how to achieve better results. Focus on the desired result, with the optimal mindset, and the correct process and tools will follow! This is why Results is positioned in the very centre of the MPTC © model.

2 - Defining Value, Seeking Perfection

"We are what we repeatedly do. Excellence, then, is not an act, but habit."

~ Aristotle

We are all very 'busy' at work. In fact we are so busy we cannot cope with the mountain of slog we have to power through on a daily basis. Have you ever worked with someone who said, "I am not busy"? We all want to feel productive. However, being busy and being productive are two very different things. So how does one measure efficiency and also productivity? First we have to define efficiency and define productivity. Then we can evaluate where we are not being effective, and eliminate waste, which stands in the way of seeking perfection for our respective process.

Efficiency

Warning! Reading and implementing this technique may change your working life for ever!

Imagine if you were to leave work on time every day from now on; would you accomplish all your daily tasks? Usually the answer is, "No, leaving at 5 pm will not be enough time to get my work done. I need to work until 9 pm."

However, you need goal posts, and thus you need a 'yard stick' to measure by. I cannot highlight this point enough. In my opinion consistently working late hours is bad for you and bad for the company. Leaving on time is one of the best ways to achieve efficiency - provided you are committed to achieving results within your newly defined time frame. You will achieve these results by improving the processes around you.

For example, let us say you are the manager of a small finance team. You have been given tight deadlines from the CFO. You feel you need another 1-2 people to ensure that the work gets completed on time. However, you know that you will not receive this as your company is reluctant to provide you with approval for two more staff. Therefore, you and your team work until 10 pm every night over the last week of the month to meet your deadline. Your management are extremely happy with the performance of your finance team and provide you with a bonus for your dedication and hard work. Are you and your team efficient at this point? Let's fast forward to three months into the future...

One of your staff hands in their resignation because they are suffering with stress and are feeling burnt out. Unfortunately this person was one of your hardest working and most efficient team members. You now realise that the amount of work the leaver was doing equated to having an additional person in your team! Training someone up to fill this gap would take a significant amount of time.

Do you now see the error? Your team was not efficient after all, as it has squandered one of its best assets. As a result, you now have four main issues:

1. You have a key member of the team who wants to leave

2.   You have a process which is hard to transfer over to new starters

3.   Your team are working late hours and as a result their efficiency is low. You will soon be suffering with low effectiveness too

4.   The micro culture has changed and your management are starting to doubt your ability to take on the additional responsibility in a promotion you have been considered for

Welcome to the point that most organisations reach before they start embracing Lean principles. We usually hit rock bottom before we realise our errors and decide to change our methodology and even our beliefs. The good news is Lean is effective, and when applied correctly it works. So how do we measure efficiency? I believe the answer is **time!**

Let us return to our story again.

You call a team meeting and everyone agrees that something needs to be done. The leaver agrees to stay at the company if they can work 8 hour shifts. You have one shot. The first action you decide to take is to measure efficiency by agreeing that **all team members must leave on time**. This is to be the new routine everyday throughout the month-end close week. If the work does not get completed then senior management will know and you will need to answer for the late and incomplete reporting. Therefore it is in your best interest to achieve results in both timeliness and accuracy.

Leaving on time has now become a benchmark to measure against. If certain tasks are not being completed on time this will help you highlight and resolve any bottleneck *(3)* issues. If your team members' performance is still not up to scratch, then there is a people training or other issue you need to address. I believe there are only two possible explanations if a team member is not completing their work:

1. Either there is something wrong with the expectations placed on that team member, or more likely, something requires correcting in the process. This is good news because it means you can take corrective action and troubleshoot *(13)* to find a solution in your process. This can be done by 'Value Stream Mapping' *(15)* which we will come to later.

2. Alternatively, there must be something wrong with the team's performance. In which case, you know that there might be training required or other investigation needs to take place in respect to staff competency. In my experience point 1 above is always the real issue. If you have solid processes then people with average competency will be able to follow them.

Nonetheless, you are now able to measure efficiency by recording the output versus the time required. You can now identify the problems which exist with your respective process and staff training requirements etc. This is a simple technique, yet it is also difficult to adhere to. Why? We are all working under social pressure at the office. Focussing on the output and achieving deadlines is an all-to-easy focus. We need to focus more on the process flow. In order to effect change we must be bold enough to change and challenge the current status. We also need to have the knowledge and confidence to drive the improvements through.

Taking small risks which potentially yield great rewards has always been a tactic which has worked for me in the past. You may fail but you will learn. If you learn, ultimately you will succeed.

Productivity and the 5 Principles of Lean

Let's go back to our story again.

As a team you have decided to leave on time but to also meet deadlines, all without a loss in quality of work. How do you then become productive?

First you decide to start with the fundamentals, the very first 5 overriding principles of Lean.

The 5 Principles of Lean

Figure 2a - 5 Principles of Lean Edited from The Five Overriding Principles Of Lean found at Cardiff University, Lean Principles

1 – Identify Customers and Specify Value: Firstly, your customers in the above example will be the senior management. These are the people to whom you provide reports in a timely and accurate manner. Now you need to define value. You do this by understanding your customers' (managements) needs and wants. What information does your management really need? In this case, it would be worth having a meeting to agree what information is important for all stakeholders in the respective month-end close process. If any part of your process exists outside what you have defined as 'customer value' then this is waste. We will come on to this shortly within the third principle of Lean.

2 – Identify and Map the Value Stream: This will be covered in much more detail later on so let us keep this in overview for now. However, do not underestimate the power of VSM (Value Stream Mapping). I have never performed this task without there being extremely favourable results.

VSM represents the analysis of the process in question, in this case our story of the month-end closing process. Each task in the process is identified, calculated and qualified. This is a visual method to help evaluate the current state (which provides a base for a future state) of the process. In the case of our story you would map the entire close process by identifying:

- Tasks performed
- People involved
- Waiting Time, Process Time, 'TAKT Time' *(12)*
- Value add and non-value add tasks

This is covered in detail later in Part II.

3 – Create Flow by Eliminating Waste: You now have a map (perhaps on the wall of your office) which you and your team are able to evaluate. In the below example, green and red represent the amount of time % spent on value add and non-value add tasks respectively.

Figure 2b – Time spent on current state process, split by value and non-value add

Your first instinct when looking at the above would be to increase the 'green' time, right? No! The principle here is to reduce the 'red' non-value adding time, thereby decreasing the total time it takes to complete the process.

Figure 2c – Time spent on future state process, split by value and non-value add

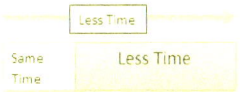

You may still spend the same amount of time adding value in both the current state and the future state process, but considerably less time spent on non-value adding tasks in the future state process. By eliminating or reducing the amount of time spent on the non-value adding tasks you are creating more 'flow' in your process. What do you think will happen when you have just freed up more time? You have just created a time gap in which to work on eliminating more waste. **Waste begets waste, but the opposite is also true when applied correctly.**

A note on mindset here; you need to be ruthless with the process. You must despise the wasteful activities. You will be challenged significantly with objections like,

"You can't do anything about that I'm afraid, Joe Bloggs over there can't get you that report any sooner... blah blah blah"

Reply: Say that you will talk with Joe Bloggs (not the most original name, granted). Find out why Joe even needs that report, and perhaps help him too by eliminating it entirely. Alternatively, find out if that report can be run before the month-end close week. External, or tasks done externally to the close process in this instance might take the same amount of time and may still be non-value adding. The ideal is to eliminate all waste. In reality, you will likely end up with a process whereby previously 0.5% of total time was value add. In the new improved process you will likely now have 10% of reduced total time attributed to value-adding tasks. This is known as the VA (Value Add) ratio. So, make sure you find out if tasks can be completed before or after your month-end week of intense deliverables. I remember this principle as an 'External/Internal' valuation. In other words, consider what unavoidable waste can be shifted 'Externally' to the respective process.

Have you not still removed a bottleneck to the close process? Do not take "no" for an answer.

"But I have always run that report, it's been asked for every month by the accounts assistant…blah blah blah"

Reply: Is the accounts assistant your customer in this case? Is this a value-adding report? What reason would the accounts assistant need this report in the first place? If it needs to be done in the close week (assuming), can this report be automated more using some standardised financial modelling? Can this be prepared before the close week?

"Unfortunately we need a better IT system; ours cannot handle this type of query… blah blah blah"

Reply: Go and talk with the IT professionals. If you have no luck then manage upwards to your seniors and tell them you have a significant bottleneck in your close process. Tell them you believe you can deliver results cheaper, faster or better if you were to find a solution. I would bet my shirt that you will find a solution and when the management are dragged into the inefficiencies of certain functional areas, people always seem to become just a little more supportive of your cause.

These objections are designed to tell you one thing; remove excuses!

4 – Respond to Customer Pull: Produce what the customer wants in a JIT (Just in Time) *(5)* fashion. Be prepared to understand your customer's (manager's) needs, and therefore already have automated ways of turning data into information using your new found skills in IT or financial modelling. The point here is to stop automatically pushing information to your management. It may not be required! In step one you would have already found out what is required, so stick to delivering value but also be prepared to be flexible to new ad-hoc requests.

If you are pushing information that is not being asked for, that is the same thing as assembling unnecessary product on the manufacturing floor and pushing it onto the next assembly box in the manufacturing process. It creates waste, it creates cost and most of all it will have a negative effect on the personnel. Producing and disseminating unnecessary information creates confusion, more questions and more reports. Again, waste will beget more waste. Respond to and be prepared for 'Pull' requests whilst aiming not to 'Push' information.

5 – Seek Perfection: You will now need to adopt continuous improvement (Kaizen *(6)*) into your process. Agree the future state process with your team members and adhere to them religiously. But also seek to eliminate more waste as time goes by. Have the mindset that the process can always be made simpler. In time you may be able to eliminate the need for the entire process! When you are given such opportunities, take them.

Excellent! From applying the 5 above principles you and your team will not only be able to close the month-end early, you will have spare time with which to review your output more thoroughly and make recommendations which will truly help senior management make the right decisions. You have now become productive.

I fully understand that you may not even work in a finance function. However, no matter what function you work within, the principles still remain the same.

3 - Spreadsheet Samurai

"Progress isn't made by early risers. It's made by lazy men trying to find easier ways to do something."

~ Robert A. Heinlein

Become Lazy

'Work smarter and not harder'. Is progressing further in your career really about how many hours you work, or is it rather about developing, and demonstrating what you are capable of? In my experience if you can set renewed processes in place that take half the time with twice the results, then this is a key sign that you are able to achieve. Therefore this is also a clear sign that you are ready to advance in your career.

However, very few of us tend to put this into practice within our daily routine. I believe the reason for this often comes down to inertia; i.e. knowing the solution but not following through. The reason is usually to do with working 'for the moment' and deciding to make do with the current processes without applying the thought and attention the problem or 'waste' requires. Our reasoning is always something like,

"I'll deal with this when I get more time",

Or,

"There is no better way of approaching this right now".

Nonetheless, it is imperative to remove these excuses, first from ourselves and then from others where applicable. One way to tackle the overpowering urge to work 'hard' rather than work 'smart' is to **become lazy**.

Is it really so bad to view a task like completing a spreadsheet template as being mundane? By becoming 'lazy' and wanting a cheaper, faster or better way of working a task, you supply the motivation to change not only the process, but also your whole attitude to working smarter. I believe it is better to be a lazy expert who **invests time** into problem solving rather than the hardest working employee in the company, who has zero time for others or even themselves. I use the word invests because that is what you will truly be doing if you dedicate time to saving time. It is a snowball effect, the more time you can save the more time you have freed up to save more time... and so on. Becoming an expert in financial modelling (particularly within a finance function) is one way to do this.

So how can financial modelling help you improve processes, timeliness, accuracy and overall better decision making? Let us take a software program most of you may already be familiar with, Microsoft Excel.

Financial Modelling – Purpose

The website wiki.answers.com defines Microsoft Excel as,

"...an electronic spreadsheet program that can be used for storing, organizing and manipulating numbers and data. It's an amazingly flexible program to find answers to logic based questions. It is a program that can compile lots of data into graphs and tables."

So what can a spreadsheet do? Please pay particular attention to the word flexible in the above quote. One of the hardest 'tricks of the trade' is to strike a balance between standardisation and flexibility. This is because the need for certain types of information requests will change over time, and often the time frame can be extremely short term. The purpose of financial modelling is to enable you to:

-        turn data into useful information
-        standardise reporting processes
-        use logic to provide calculations
-        use programming to automate processes
-        other various useful purposes

Therefore, the main purpose of financial modelling is to combine most or all of the above benefits in order to produce analysis which will lead to decision making and therefore corrective action. Financial modelling can involve a human user inputting criteria or data, and the model will perform automatic calculations to provide you with best defined information, such as KPI's *(8)*, as the output.

An example might be a sales report which allows a user to import data with 10,000 lines. It then summarises the data by sales person. On the summary, you have the ability to drill down further into, say, customer. Then perhaps more information could be added such as Sales ROI (Return on Investment) metrics, or colour coding for poor or excellent performance etc.

Now compare the above example with someone who manually goes through 10,000 lines of data and with a highlighter pen and a calculator. They manually add up sales by person and do not have time to add up the other information. This is a rather basic example, but I am confident you now understand the essential purpose of a financial model.

Financial Modelling – Function

So how does this all work? We will cover this in a lot more detail later on. However, the basic functions are shown below, and are all extremely powerful. We will look at some brief examples.

1 - Spreadsheet "functions": Functions are certain commands that when typed into a cell produce an output. For example, the below is a "SUM" function written in a given 'cell'. This will sum up the total of all the sales by everyone combined and will total £30,209 in cell reference "C7".

Figure 3a – SUM Formula

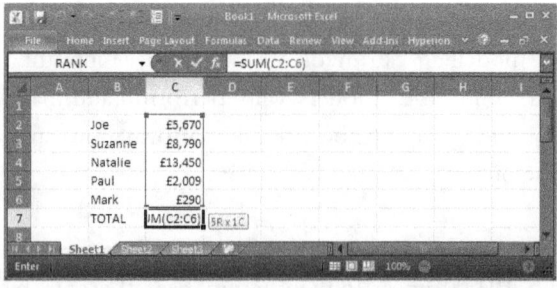

The next illustration will show you a "SUMIF" function (AKA 'formula'). This will sum from the previous data too. Only this time it will only sum information in respect to "Suzanne" and thus will return a value of £8,790 in the cell reference "F2".

Figure 3b – SUMIF Formula

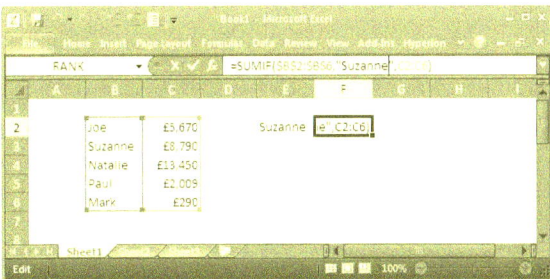

2 - PivotTables: This allows you to 'drag and drop' summarised data into a report enabling you to see information split by rows, columns and filters in any way that you choose. Either in chart format or table format. This is extremely useful when looking to analyse data at a high level and then be able to drill into detail when required. We will create a PivotTable in Part III.

Figure 3c – PivotTable

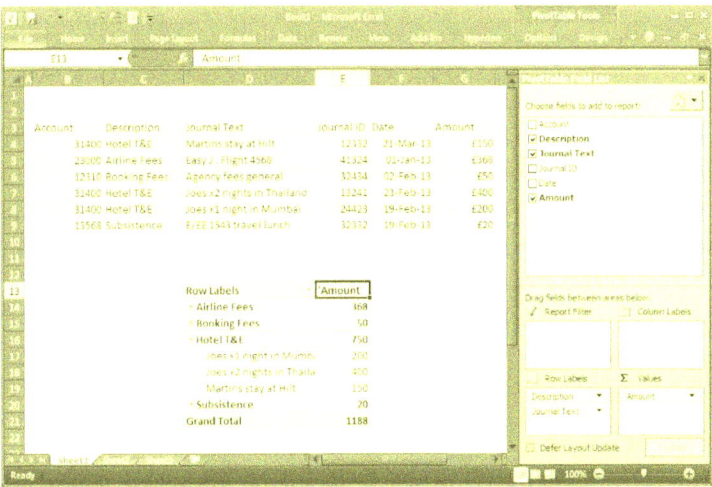

The above figure shows the basic principle behind a PivotTable. Rows 3-9 show an example of what a data table might look like. In this example we are looking at a snapshot of travel related spend within an organisation. The lower section of the sheet shows the PivotTable. To the right of this is the PivotTable Field List. This is where you can drag and drop certain criteria in order to filter the items you want to see. In this case we have shown the account description and journal text as rows with the amount to be summarised. This way you could drill down further just by clicking.

For example, if you were to click on the "Hotel T&E" cross sign; you would see all the describing items which contributed to the £750.

Can you imagine if the underlying data extended to nearly 700,000 rows instead of just 6 as shown above? Yet you can automatically see the same summarisation of data irrespective of how many rows there are. The information will still be calculated for you. You can still standardise and summarise the view in the same format desired irrespective of how many rows of data there are.

3 - Macros: This is more advanced, but the principles still remain. Put simply, you can record certain movements that you make when using your spreadsheet and then have Excel re-run these for you whenever you require it to. Think of it this way; imagine you have to wash your car every Sunday. Well, you decide this Sunday to wash your car with extra care and have an automated robot take notes on every action you take in doing so. Then every Sunday you push a button and tell your robot to wash the car. It will do so exactly how you did. You have saved 1 hour for every Sunday to come. **Automation is Key**.

Now let us apply a real scenario. Let us say that every week you receive a report from Joe Bloggs whereby you are always required to hide columns Z, AA, AB, AR, EY and PT as well as rows 52, 99, 102 and 300.

You are then required to copy the prior month section of the spreadsheet and paste its values into a new sheet within the same workbook. You then need to colour the total line black and have the text as white as well as make the headings bold.

Firstly, I would like to point out that this type of task should always prompt you to look further into why you have to do this. But let's assume for the moment there is a valid reason.

So you decide to record yourself doing this one more time. You hide the columns and rows, copy the data you need and paste it into the relevant sheet. You then make it look nice with bold headings and totals as before. This took 20 minutes in total. Once you have finished recording, you assign a keyboard shortcut. This means that whenever you hit some keys within the workbook, Excel will repeat everything you just did exactly as you did it before. Just like the robot that washes your car! (If you find such a robot, be sure to email me straight away!)

The following week, Joe sends you a new report and you open it. You then hit some shortcut keys on your keyboard and all of a sudden before your very eyes everything is done for you automatically. Congratulations, you just saved yourself 20 minutes per week. Now use that time to automate more processes - and also don't forget to ask Joe why on earth this report is not already presented correctly to start with.

Remember there is no point in having a process if you don't need to. In fact, why not check with senior management if they even use this report at all and perhaps you can persuade Joe to let you help him develop a model which runs with greater efficiency and contains more relevant information. I cannot stress enough how real this type of scenario is. You need to look for the opportunities and always question "why". I am sure there are vastly more time consuming processes that you are probably already facing which could be automated better. Remember as a bonus that robust automation also reduces the scope for human error.

Therefore, by automating you are now able to perform tasks more quickly as well as achieving greater accuracy in your reporting.

4 - Visual Basic for Applications (VBA): Programming within Excel's VBA is much like the above macro example. Except it is slightly more advanced in the sense that it involves creating code, or editing code within Excel's programming module. If you would like to see what this looks like, open Excel on your computer and hit "ALT + F11". You will see a window which looks something like this:

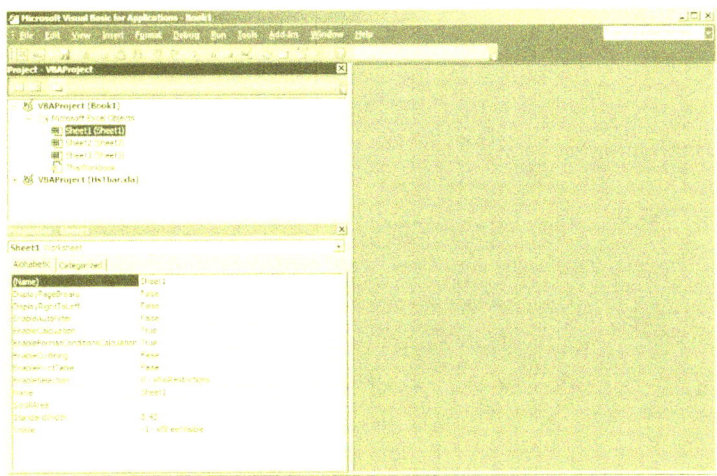

This will open up the 'VB (Visual Basic) Editor' window for you and will provide an overall view of how this looks. It is highly recommended that you first become a super user of spreadsheets without needing the use of VBA. **You do not have to become greatly advanced**. You just need to become very good at employing the fundamentals and being creative. Then, when you feel more confident, I highly recommend repeating the same learning process, only this time after learning the fundamentals of VBA. It will pay dividends in the long run.

I believe that in respect to data any logical process can be automated (whether it is in the format of numbers, text or dates). This means that if you work a process within a spreadsheet, even if it is just manually changing rows etc., if there is logic behind what you are doing you can get the system to work for you. This is done by programming the same logic you use with your own brain. There are countless examples of this being true and I am yet to be proven wrong.

So from now on every time you use a spreadsheet please ask yourself, "Is there logic to what I am doing right now?" If the answer is yes, then you can absolutely have the spreadsheet working for you in the future. And if the standard process changes, you can be flexible enough to change your programming logic.

The above examples are limited, and there are many more functions and tools which will improve your working life when using spreadsheets. Just remember that spreadsheets can be a process as well as a tool. Once you open Pandora's Box, there is no going back. You will achieve great satisfaction from making your working life easier and having systems work for you. You will also probably catch the 'continuous improvement bug' once you have learnt some basic financial modelling.

To summarise, become 'lazy' in your approach to tasks and automate them. Become ultra-efficient at using the fundamentals of spreadsheets and other systems. From doing this not only will you improve your processes and working life, but you will also improve that of the other people around you. Just maintain a mindset to continuously learn!

PART II: Out with the Old, In with the New

4 – Cleaning Out Your Closet with '5S'

"Tell me and I will forget, show me and I may remember, involve me and I'll understand."

~ Chinese Proverb

"And this is how you 5S your office," said our Lean leadership trainer on a three week intensive Lean training course. There were images showing staplers labelled with their owners' names and tape markers on staff desks showing "where the scissors belong". 5S in the office meant sorting your paper work, setting new layout standards in order, keeping everything neat, standardising the layout by taping markers for where things belong, and finally, putting an emphasis on sustaining this practice. That was all there was to office 5S, but that is not what we are going to talk about here.

You see there may have been a time, where we were not so computer literate, when papers would fly all over the place and the office risked becoming an inefficient hazard. However, "5S on the production floor" meant so much more than its cousin "5S in the office". Just having a neat desk will not in itself make us super-efficient in the office, helpful though it may be.

Back to my story. I was staring something momentous yet obvious right in the face and I had to speak up. I realised that there is so much hidden waste in information flow around the administrative environment. Perhaps because information is intangible, you will find very little guidance on how to handle it efficiently. But when you realise the importance of organising your information flow you will be astounded.

As discussed earlier in this book, it is vital to understand the relationship between Product and Information. Almost everything to do with product flow can be replicated in information flow. This applies to 5S too. And once you take this fact on board, it will radically improve your data handling process.

What is 5S?

There are many minor variations of what constitutes 5S. I find that the website operational-excellence-consulting.com sums this up very well:

1.   Sort (Seiri)
2.   Set-in-Order (Seiton)
3.   Shine (Seiso)
4.   Standardise (Seiketsu)
5.   Sustain (Shitsuke)

Sort

In the workshop Sort relates to getting rid of hazards or waste, and sorting items within your given area. Here you will want to identify tools which are more useful than others. Get rid of any tools, boxes or debris etc. which you don't need, and remove from the area anything unrelated to the process at hand.

There are many variations on how to do this practically, but let us see if we can identify a few ways to approach this in the admin environment.

#1: What reports do you still need to run on a monthly basis? I am sure there are many reports you will come across from time to time whereby management previously requested you provide something on a periodic basis, that you no longer need to provide but still do. One way to eradicate as much non-necessary reporting is via the process of 'Red Tagging' *(11)*.

In the production world, this means putting a red sticker or tag on every single item in the warehouse. Every time you use an item simply remove the tag. After 30 days evaluate what items still have the red tag attached. These will likely be items which you no longer use and can be sold for scrap or put further away from the items you use more frequently (if they are still needed at all). So how do you apply this to the world of information flow? Well, you may not agree with what I am about to tell you but here is an approach I have taken which has paid dividends; Do the 'Red Tagging' process in reverse. That's right, take a risk. Other than the critical reports which you yourself directly discuss with management, stop providing all other information for 30 days. That's it. Either someone will desperately need the information and contact you for it - in which case you can sheepishly reply and submit it if necessary - or no one will contact you, and thus I can almost guarantee it was not useful, not necessary, and certainly not analysis which could be used for decision making.

Of course many people would prefer not to take this approach. However, you will be surprised at how much work we accumulate which is waste. We feel that waste may be important, but how confident are we that the company will be better off for any given report? If the company needs this information, it will ask for it. In this case you will know what is required and why it adds value.

Very often the issue of providing reporting which is unnecessary disappears when people leave a company. I have witnessed people who work until midnight regularly due to overload of work requirements, only to find that their new starting replacement has far less to do. Why is this? It happens because when a new person joins the company and there is no job procedure manual or hand-over, they only perform critical tasks and drop the rest of the non-value adding tasks which the predecessor would perform by accumulation.

#2 Ask: Ask people,

"Are there reports you run which you are not sure are necessary?"

Find out from others in your team if there are any reports of uncertain value. I remember setting up a SharePoint site to do this. Users all around the globe would submit reports to SharePoint with a description of how long it takes to run the report and who they send it to. If you don't know what SharePoint is, just think of it as a way to share information on the company intranet.

Before I go any further with this story, please note time is money. We are usually paid fixed salaries; everything you spend your time on carries a cost.

Ok, to continue. Once we had the SharePoint site set up, a member from a local business unit submitted a query, "We run these two reports and it takes two days, please help". When I called the person who raised this red flag I asked,

> "What does this report get used for?"

To which I received the response,

> "I don't know exactly."

I immediately called the person to whom the mysterious reports were submitted. Their response was to tell me that they just save the report in their drive because that was what they were told to do when they joined the company.

Utter madness. I called my colleague, who raised the query in the first place, and said,

> "Stop running this report with immediate effect! There is no value in doing this."

They were only too delighted to be saved from two days of compiling unnecessary reports. Did anyone shout for this missing report? No!

By now I am sure you can realise how important the **Sort** aspect of 5S can be to not only you, but to your surrounding team as well.

Set-in-Order

This is commonly referred to as a method for setting workshop items into their most ideal location. Given their particular process flow path, this creates ease and efficiency of access.

However, in the world of information there are of course a few applications too:

#1 Automated Data: This is where you can assign every report to automatically save to a certain area on your drive, set and save favourites in your IT system for quick access to data, and speak with IT professionals who can automate data to run periodically for you and save this in your local file system.

#2 File Order: You can also use this principle to adjust your file structure with an underscore '_' before the name of each file or folder which you access the most often. This will ensure that the folders you reference the most will be nearer the top of the file structure for quick access.

#3 The 20 Second Rule: What is the 20 second rule? If someone new joins the company and you give them access to your file structure, could they navigate to any particular file within 20 seconds of needing to? Your file structure needs to be self-evident and represent a logical order. If a stranger can find the respective file within 20 seconds without assistance, you have succeeded!

#4 Job procedure manuals: Make sure that every single task or tool you have is documented with adequate instructions. Each team member should have their own tasks assigned to them which are clearly defined in a manual. They should also each be responsible for creating a job procedure manual for each respective new task they complete. These should be saved in a shared and easily accessible location. If you do not have job procedures for your own tasks then create them. When you have to hand over work to somebody, you have potentially just saved hours of having to explain yourself twice. Preparation to avoid your time being required is far too underrated.

I am sure you can think of a few more examples yourself. Please take a moment to consider how much time just the first two 5S' will save you.

Shine

In a workshop environment, having dirt, grease and other waste on product and machinery can often hide a latent problem. If you have machinery which is brightly painted and well maintained, when a leak occurs this will become highly visible.

The same principle can be applied to your reporting within spreadsheets. You should have check formulas on all your spreadsheets. There should be no non-standard calculations or text saved on reports which are not of any value to the user or end customer. A neat spreadsheet with "IF" checks, conditional formatting for errors and consistency in format, will be a great asset in assuring accuracy. Just like when a machine springs a leak, data can also sometimes prove inconsistent; if you have the pre-checks already set up with visual signs of potential errors, then you will be in a stronger position to trust your model and identify potential data issues early on.

This will also help you to develop trust in using spreadsheets, if you are currently apprehensive about doing so. I have never had an issue with the program. Every time I have stumbled upon spreadsheet errors they have always been human error related. As the old saying goes, "A bad workman blames his tools."

Standardise

The same applies here as it does to production. You need to have standard processes which are adhered to and only changed if the process can be made better, or indeed entirely removed.

This is an obvious one. However, I would like to add the word "streamline" to possibly make a 6th 'S'. This can be accomplished through financial modelling. Have you ever wondered whether it is possible to have the same data populate several different reports for several different users, instead of just one report for one user? Once you have a standard process, coupled with some financial modelling 'know how', you can set up reports to literally almost 100% run themselves through linking functions and formulas to data. Much of this will be covered in the final part of this book. However, it is important once again to realise that having system skills can be very useful.

Sustain

The improvements outlined above need to be maintained to be worthwhile. Here is an example. My manager and I had put the whole team together to process map and set in place the 5S principles within a finance department. Within a week we had managed to bring their month-end close process forward two days, and for a while none of the staff worked weekends anymore. Two months later I was to discover that everyone had just reverted back to the old process and became stuck in their old ways once again. So what had happened?

Well, one by one the staff fell back into the same old 'working for the now' mentality and did not do the pre-month-end preparation work that they had implemented previously. They had stopped believing in working smarter and became overwhelmed again by the onslaught brought on by themselves and senior management requirements. They had stopped looking to leave on time and not work weekends, and thus become slaves once more to the old process.

There was no longer a process of standardisation with the ability to be flexible. There are also issues with people approaching Lean as an individual journey. This is a 'team sport'. It is not about you. It is about your team and the moment we forget that, it will be difficult to support one another when times get tough.

Sustain is commonly seen as one of the more difficult aspects of 5S. But sustaining a newly created process is pivotal to success. It is pointless to inject an improved process as a 'one off' type event and then revert back to the same old wasteful activities. You need to ensure that you and your team are fully committed, and that you want positive change. You need to get involved and live in the mindset of 5S. New problems will often arise and you will need to be slick in your current approach to processes, in order to allow time for combating these challenges.

5 - Value Stream Mapping: A Powerful Tool

"Where there is no standard there can be no Kaizen."

~ Taiichi Ohno

There was barely a moment to lose. I had just landed at Marco Polo airport, Venice, and on getting out the taxi my colleague and I were escorted into a room no more than about two square metres in size. We were told that all the other rooms were booked out. This Italian business had just been acquired by our company, and the local finance department employees were not happy about us coming along to change things.

There were to be no excuses and no setbacks. The previous month-end had been hell. The Italian financial planning team had worked non-stop and suffered late nights through a full week of month-end carnage. Remember, waste begets waste. When results rolled in late and unexpected, more questions arose from senior management and thus more time was spent by the Italian finance team to seek answers. Finally, the added cost of sending my colleague and me out to investigate sounded the alarm bells. The process simply had to change.

We arrived in the office and had a brief meeting with the local Finance Director.

"We need to close our books earlier, then we can be more prepared for the forecast process and our variances won't be so large and unexplainable next time," he said.

"Excellent", we replied, and before you knew it we had cleared the room of all the clutter we could. Except for the delicious Italian biscuits. They had to stay.

What is Value Stream Mapping (VSM)?

Around five seconds later, my colleague and I started tearing off large sheets of flip chart paper and taping them to the wall with yellow masking tape. I had asked one of the staff members if she wouldn't mind supplying three packs of sticky 'Post-It' notes and different colour pens.

"Why?!" she asked.

"Because, we are going to eat some Italian biscuits and fix the 'Actuals Month-End Close' process using Value Stream Mapping", I replied.

Without asking any questions she obliged, and soon we had a top member of the finance team as well as the FD helping us to add sticky notes on the flip chart paper, as a method for mapping out the entire finance month-end close process.

The wall looked something like this:

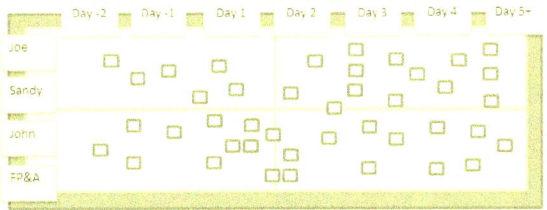

The large notes at the top represented the days of 'month-end close' and the rows of notes represented departments or people. The yellow notes represented the steps that were performed by the department/person on a particular month-end day. We would write the description of the task on each note, along with a few other factors to be covered shortly.

So, aside from the biscuits, what were the benefits of our session acting like children by drawing and sticking things on the wall? Let me tell you; if you want to change a process you will often need to be highly visual. Waste needs to be made visible in a way everyone, speaking any language, can understand. Then no one can argue with your methodology, and everyone can understand the key issues. So make it self-evident where the flaws in the process are by using this visual method.

The benefits of taking this approach to VSM are as follows:

• **Visibility:** By having a large set of tasks laid out in such an obvious fashion, you will soon receive an awakening otherwise known as the 'ah-ha effect'. This is when a sudden realisation of the errors and constraints comes to light.

• **Attention:** People literally sit up and pay attention. They become intrigued, and therefore get involved.

• **Clarity:** You will be able to see an entire process laid out and therefore identify the bottlenecks which are preventing you from achieving results. VSM provides a visual methodology for identifying and correcting your current state process.

• **Identification:** The reason we use sticky notes is so that we can move tasks around with ease. When interpreting tasks in a process, we are not always correct the first time. When then consulting with the task performer they might say, "No, that is not what I do, it works like this..." In which case, you can unstick the note and re-stick is somewhere more applicable. Or replace it with a new note which represents the description of the task more accurately.

• **Documentation:** It is easy to transfer the end information to a spreadsheet (or other form of document) for recording and measuring. Imagine writing down a whole process on just a note pad. Would you be able to identify all the process flaws? I feel strongly on this point. To reach Kaizen (continuous improvement) we need to be able to have easy visibility of self-evident information. We should not rely on understanding a process through jotting down notes.

• **Building Future State:** As you will learn shortly VSM is not just about mapping the current process. Once this is done and measurements are made you can then map the future state process. This is usually much quicker as waste will be reduced. I have experienced using around 10% of 'current state process' sticky notes, in order to rebuild a 'future state process'. This means that 90% of tasks were waste and therefore disposed of.

• **Sharing:** Remember Lean is not about you. It is a 'team sport'. I find the best ideas are usually formulated by the ground runners, the people who understand each task inside out. True Lean leadership and Lean facilitation means tapping into the creativity and genius found in others. VSM is a way of providing all participants with clarity so that they can see the challenges and solutions for themselves. Welcome to the fun part of VSM; harnessing the creativity of others.

So, after reading all of these snippets and seeing its potential, you are probably what exactly is VSM? The website Wikipedia.com will tell you that VSM is a "technique used to analyse and design the flow of materials and information required to bring a product or service to a consumer."

You will need to use the ten steps below as a checklist for providing a successful VSM exercise:

☐   Define and Document a Business Case

☐   Assemble a Lean Team, Delegate Tasks

☐   Identify Scope, Identify Value, Know Your Customer

☐   Organise the 'Meeting'

☐   Calculate TAKT Time

☐   Start the Exercise!

☐   Highlight Value, Bottlenecks and Rework

☐   Document Process Time and Waiting Time

☐   Document Suggestions on Effort-Benefit Matrix

☐   Repeat for Future State, Assign Actions and Follow Up

Define and Document a Business Case

Let's assume you have identified a need for change. Now you, the change agent, need to facilitate an exercise to identify the optimum process of creating flow without waste for your customer. Remember your customer can be senior management, your colleagues or an actual customer.

This type of activity will cost you and others time and therefore will have a financial cost associated with it. Remember - if you have eight hours to chop down a tree spend the first seven hours sharpening the axe! The more prepared you are the better you will understand the current process and help implement an outstanding new one. So prepare a strong and compelling business case to send to your managers, Lean team and colleagues. It must create a sense of urgency and ensure that people take you seriously. Remember to clearly state your reasons for creating the business case, and suggest the possible benefits for having a more streamlined process.

Note: Try to avoid using your businesses capital or using 'spending money' as a problem solving solution. If this is where you are heading then you are perhaps not using your team and creative mind to the full extent.

Assemble a Lean Team / Delegate Tasks

You will need a team. Your team must have the same goal as you; to improve a process. A team of four is recommended, and you can delegate tasks as follows:

1.   The documenter/time keeper
2.   The scribe

3.   The facilitator (you)

4.   The driver

When choosing a high performing team, try not to only recruit people who are already familiar with the process. An outsider will often be the one who asks the question "why". If possible, you should also ask people in the organisation who have a proven track record in improving processes.

The facilitator, you, is the person who holds the team and exercise together - the 'glue' of the operation. You need to make sure all team members and participants are staying on track. You also need to be aware of 'scope creep', ensuring that you are not breaking the bounds of what the business case covers.

The driver needs to be inquisitive and good at extracting detailed information from people who will be 'cagey' about relinquishing the elements of what it is they do, or how it is that a certain task is performed.

The scribe will need to be able to follow conversation and absorb detail. They will be writing on sticky notes and posting tasks etc. on the wall.

The documenter must have sufficient skills on Microsoft or other relevant applications. They will be formulating the presentation, reports and recommendations for you to distribute at a later time. This is important. When your team achieve results you must take pride in presenting and articulating the outcome.

Identify Scope, Identify Value, Know Your Customer

Identifying Scope: Identifying the scope of a process usually means the end-to-end process you wish to examine. For example, if you were to analyse the process of producing a weekly sales report, how much of the process would you wish to examine? You could start right from customer quotation, all the way to the end user receiving progress reports.

Identifying the scope is important because you need to manage time in the VSM process, as well as obtain information relevant to the process you are investigating. You need to be wary of 'scope creep'. This happens very easily and can steer you off course. Scope creep occurs when discussions get extended into issues outside the boundaries of what you have decided to analyse. This can end up swamping you with facts which are not relevant to your overall process evaluation.

Identifying Value: Whilst performing the VSM analysis, you need to be clear on which tasks are value adding and which tasks are not. As described earlier your goal is not to increase the amount of time spent on value adding tasks. For example, if a process takes two hours to complete and only one hour is spent actually adding value, the aim of improving the process is not to spend five hours adding value and five hours on 'wasteful' steps. No, the aim is to spend one hour completing the task in total (the value adding time). Of course this is not usually realistic because eliminating all wasteful tasks is an impossible ideal. However, the point is that you need to reduce the total time spent on a given task not increase the value adding proportion as discussed earlier in Part I. This is the very point which will enable you to work fewer hours to achieve better results, and thus help you become more efficient and productive.

So how does one identify value? There are many different examples of what value truly means. However, let me guide you through thinking about value from the right point of view... the customer's point of view.

In the process which you are analysing, who is your customer? In the example of producing a sales report above, the customer is the end user. Now, imagine that your customer is paying you. What is your customer paying for? When you are making a product it's easy to answer - the customer is paying you to change the shape or form of materials so that it provides them with the desired output, the product.

In the sales report example there is no physical good being supplied. Instead your manager (the customer) is requiring information to help them with decision making. So value is formed from taking data (raw material) and turning it into information (product). Any time the data has to be worked on by changing its form is defined as a value adding step. For example, if you have 1,000 rows of data for five particular sales people showing their sales made in a given month, and you sum this up in total by person, this would be a value adding step in a process.

Be aware of the difference between value and rework! If you have to change the data to provide the correct sales output because the data is wrong then this is rework, not value. If you have to sum the information up by sales person more than once, this again is rework.

Know Your Customer: Usually the value adding tasks are by far the quickest to perform. Often we spend much more time correcting and manipulating data than ought to be necessary, and much less time focussing on our customers' benefit.

In business if you please the customer you will do well and earn bigger profits. The same is true internally. You will have a stronger chance of progressing when focussing on delivering exceptional results to management and colleagues, who are your customers. Conversely, the opposite is also true. **If you do not provide a fast, reliable and effective service you will try to make up for this by working more hours**. We all have a tendency to fall into this trap. Before you know it you will become a process problem by making yourself 'indispensable'. This is a warning sign to management. Therefore, focus on what is value and deliver this to the customer in abundance wherever possible in a standardised manner.

Organise the Meeting

This does not need much explanation, but you must ensure that everyone in your team and VSM attendees are available, and are also fully committed to supporting the business case.

This is often overlooked, and can render your exercise useless when it comes to the punch. Sometimes people aren't available because 'they are too busy'. If you have developed a strong business case and obtained buy-in from stakeholders, this should not be an excuse. Remove excuses!

Finally, you will need to ensure you have adequate stationary such as flip chart paper, sticky notes, different colour pens, masking tape, computers and food. Food is important as you a will wish to cover as much as you can in the given time. Value Stream Mapping can be exhausting and you need to ensure that everybody is staying sharp on the job. Otherwise you may not get the level of creative problem solving you had hoped for.

Calculate TAKT Time

Goal posts are vital to keeping everyone on track. It is all too easy to say, "We will have to accept doing this task, there is no other way." You cannot accept any task in your future state process if it does not fall within your criteria. You need to know your boundaries and goals. Having goal posts will ensure that you are constantly aware of what your bottlenecks are and where your major challenges lie.

One goal which is important is your TAKT Time. The website theleanthinker.com will provide this calculation to you as:

Available Minutes for Production / Required Units of Production = TAKT Time

All you need to do is tweak this calculation for your own purpose. When we were examining the Italian month-end close process the TAKT Time formula would look like this:

Available minutes over month-end close / required number of tasks to complete for Corporate Accounting = TAKT Time

TAKT Time will highlight the maximum time which you have available to spend on any given task. If a task's processing time goes over the TAKT Time then you have not reached your goal.

Whilst adding this task to the current state map just mark it with a colour, shape, or anything which you have defined as representing a block or 'bottleneck'. Any task which stands in the way of you reaching your goal should be marked, and targeted for obliterating.

Start the Exercise!

By now I am sure you are becoming familiar with how this process works. By completing the above few steps you are now ready to start your Value Stream Mapping exercise.

Take action and get started. You can do this by taping flip chart paper to the wall and getting the people with the knowledge you need into the room. Start by reconfirming what you are here for and why this is important. The driver will need to ask questions like,

> "So you work in Accounts Payable?"

> "When closing the ledger for AP, what is the very first thing you do? Please take us through this in detail carefully"

> "Can we have a copy of that report summary?"

Whenever a new task is mentioned by an interviewee, write it down on a sticky note and put it on the wall aligning it to the columns and rows you have defined. In our Italian month-end process map earlier, we defined rows as functions/people and columns as 'month-end close' days.

Nonetheless one discussion will lead to another and before you know it, you will have a whole network of tasks to discuss, track and evaluate.

Highlight Value, Bottlenecks and Rework

Any tasks which add value, are a bottleneck or involve rework should be given a colour coding or require highlighting. The purpose is to make key activities visible.

I would suggest highlighting with green pen (or using a green sticky note) any task which involves adding value. Bottlenecks should be colour coded red and rework can be given a star and/or coloured orange. The types of colour coding or markers you use are not important in themselves; what is important is that you have visible meanings on your mapping which draw attention to specific 'problem children'.

Document Process Time and Waiting Time

Process time is the time required to complete a task. If you spend five hours running a report, but only 30 minutes saving, opening and editing the report, your process time is 30 minutes and your waiting time is five hours.

The scribe should write the process time on the bottom right hand corner of each sticky note and the waiting time on the bottom left hand corner. Why is waiting time important? Waiting time can be a bottleneck in itself. If a report takes five hours to run and you can only run it on a specific date then you may have to consider having an IT engineer automate this to happen overnight for you or find another way of getting the data you need.

At the end of the current state process map mark down the VA (value-add) Ratio dividing the time spent processing value add tasks by the time taken working on wasteful tasks. I usually find the VA ratio ends up between 0.5% - 2.0% for a current state process.

Once you have completed the future state process as described later on, repeat the same cycle again. What is the total time spent on processing tasks now versus previously? What is your VA ratio now compared with before? You should see an improvement.

Document Suggestions on Effort-Benefit Matrix

The most important aspect of doing this exercise is not just to understand what's causing problems. It is to change the process for the better! It is vital that you contribute and capture creative problem solving suggestions whilst mapping the current state process. There are three reasons for this:

1. You might forget them

2. You want to avoid discussing the future process until the current process has been fully mapped out

3. You want to start building up an arsenal of points to refer back to which will serve as your action plan items and recommendations

4. Most importantly, these suggestions will serve to improve the process. This is the whole point of VSM whereby you want to create flow and develop a robust process which average people can follow. So capture the suggestions which can help you do this!

The way to capture creative suggestions is to have a flip chart board nearby and to draw an Effort-Benefit Matrix.

To do this, first draw four quadrants. Then draw an arrow across the page on the x axis and another arrow adjacent on the y axis. Mark the x axis arrow as "Effort" and the y axis arrow as "Benefit".

Your flipchart should look something like this:

Figure 5b – Effort Benefit Matrix

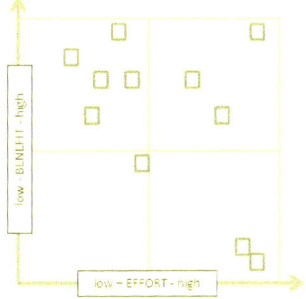

 Whenever an idea is given, the scribe should write this on a sticky note and assign it to the matrix. If the idea will provide you with a high benefit and will be low effort to achieve then this idea should be placed in the top left hand quadrant. If the suggestion will have a high benefit but take a high amount of effort then this should be placed in the top right hand section of the quadrant.

The above method will enable you to evaluate which actions should be given the highest priority. Those in the top left hand quadrant should be tackled first and then those in the top right. Finally, you can tackle the bottom left and bottom right last.

Repeat for Future State and Follow Up

By now, you and your team will have a solid idea about how things should work and how to achieve success in your new process! If you do not at this point, then you may want to rethink your suggestions and continue asking questions as well as brainstorming ideas for removing bottlenecks and 'waste' activities. Where there is a will to do so, there is always a way.

Now that you have an idea of how the process should work, go and build a new map. Remember, before tearing down the old one you will need to make sure each task has been documented, detailing process time, waiting time, value adding tasks, bottlenecks and rework. The new map should be put up on the wall and should meet all your objective requirements. Be sure to speak with other stakeholders to get their input and buy-in as to whether they believe in the new process.

Once you have agreement, assign actions and report on your progress. Then be sure to follow up periodically. What is the reason for this? It is unbelievably easy to fall back into old habits. Remember the story about the finance staff that was able to stop working weekends through completing the VSM exercise? Soon, they returned to the same habits and were forced to be slaves to the old process once more. Be sure to assign a champion to the process. Choose someone who can be held accountable for sustaining flow.

Final Word on VSM

I am yet to have worked on mapping a process whereby the results didn't bring dramatic improvement. You need to try using this tool in order to believe in its effectiveness. Start with a process which is small and fairly easy to understand. Once you see the power of VSM, you will be able to add this to your continuous improvement arsenal. **Better processes involve less time. Less time plus more productivity equals a better work-life balance.**

If you apply this to your own processes asking others for help and insight, I feel very confident that you will reduce your working hours dramatically. By focussing on performing a fantastic service for your customer you will build solid credibility which will help you advance safely (without added stress and working hours) in your career.

6 - Starting with Mindset

"A good head and a good heart are always a formidable combination."

~ Nelson Mandela

Whilst travelling in South Africa and trying to figure out what I wanted to do with my life my uncle asked me,

"What are you good with Shaun?"

To which I paused for a moment and replied,

"I tell you what I am not good with Uncle Mike… one, Money and two, Women"

Uncle Mike was a well renowned ENT specialist and an extremely talented painter. I had (and still have) tremendous respect for him. Slightly concerned by my response he went into his study and came back with two books. The first book was "Men Are from Mars, Women Are from Venus" by relationship counsellor, John Gray, and the second was "Rich Dad, Poor Dad", by investor and business man, Robert T. Kiyosaki.

"Shaun, you can borrow one of these books whilst you are travelling, which one would you like?" said Uncle Mike.

…I opted for Robert T. Kiyosaki's book, "Rich Dad, Poor Dad". Even now, I sometimes wonder how my life would have been if I had chosen the other book…

There is a reason I am sharing this with you. Robert T. Kiyosaki's book changed the course of my life and who I would become, due to the simple instruction, "Be-Do-Have".

In order to achieve and "have" the results you want, you need to "do" the things which will get you there. You can only achieve doing by "being" in the mindset of the type of person who you need to become. Therefore, all change surely has to start from your mindset. So, as the saying goes,

"If you want things to change, you have to change."

Attitude

One of my first managers, a Finance Director and business owner said, "If you have a good attitude, you are 90% there."

To this day I believe this message to be one of the truest in my life,

"The worst disability in life is a bad attitude."
— Supa Nova Slom

A good attitude can help you with your beliefs. Therefore it can provide you with a starting point in rising to the challenge. A bad attitude disarms you. It takes away your ability to effect change. We all suffer from stress sometimes, and this can cause us to view the world or our environment in a negative light. It is therefore Key that you focus your energy on believing that solutions and change are possible. Having this attitude will help you fend off negative feedback, improper criticism and challenges that say, "This approach will not work."

Remember that not everyone will agree with your initiatives, or even your motives. Many will doubt that you are going to achieve results. You need to be self-motivated, driven, energised and positive in your daily life. The way to accomplish all these is to believe that you can effect positive change. This will give you the energy to do the things you need to in order to obtain your desired results.

> "What we believe is what we see."
>
> — Sukant Ratnakar, Open the Windows

Belief is powerful. You need to believe in your own learning ability and also your ability to effect change. Having confidence is what will often set you apart from your colleagues, and as you make changes and achieve results your confidence will grow - and so will your teams. You need to start somewhere. Start by believing in yourself.

You and Your Organisation

First, I would like to make myself unpopular by saying the following; it is not about you. Lean is not about you. By being efficient and productive you will reap the benefits of having more time, more prospects and better development. This is great. But it should not be your only reason for self-development. It is important to be aware that you are not entitled to your job. My job, your job and everyone else's job exists because your respective business makes money or is government funded etc. Either way, there is always a 'customer' involved. If we soak up cost and do not add value for our customer, then we cannot claim to deserve the privilege of having a job.

We owe it to the company to push for success, because then we too will be successful, and we will be protecting our own job as well as other people's jobs. Before I go on, think about what a company is. In your mind is the 'company' associated with the management? Wrong. The company means you and those around you. So when I say 'we owe it to the company' what I really mean is that you owe it to yourself and fellow colleagues to drive effectiveness.

Remember that a company or entity is seen as a legal 'person'. It is people working processes which makes up the company, not products or customers. The product is the function for satisfying the customer who funds the cycle. The very same cycle which keeps us employed.

So remember 'the company' means you, others and the processes you manage. Support your company because by doing so you will be supporting yourself and others. This in turn will help you to keep maintaining a positive attitude, particularly when the 'chips are down'.

Managing Upwards

We mentioned this previously in respect to identifying value and meeting your customer's (usually your manager's) needs. Sometimes management do not always have the answers. In seeking the answers they might ask for several reports or several new processes to be put in place so that they have the information they need to support effective decision making. All of us, including senior management, are people. We are human and therefore fallible and do not always have the optimal answer.

However, usually we are by nature cautious about challenging management, and run the risk of becoming 'Yes' people and never saying 'No' to a request. Sometimes though, management requirements fail to add value to an overall process. The challenge here is to correct for this. Now I am not saying to tell your boss, "You are creating havoc with this new delivery report process, it makes no sense and you are clearly being an idiot!" Although I am sure at times you may have felt like saying this, there can be a much more constructive approach…

The first advice is **take the initiative**. If you are being asked for several reports and cannot see the value of them, have you thought about running another process alongside this yourself? One which is faster and provides management with more useful information? By doing this you are not only showing initiative and the ability to effect positive change, but you are also giving your customer more than they paid for. And in return you can request that the old process be made redundant, to allow you to continue providing more exceptional reporting. Who could say no?

Another suggestion is to talk with your management and ask, "What are you aiming at achieving by requesting this?" Your manager has a goal and needs a particular result. In having this requirement, they have come up with a request which they believe will fill the need. More often than not management will need to refine this request and repeatedly ask for add-on tasks which will cause you to work additional hours in order to provide reworked information. By asking your manager what result they are trying to achieve you can put yourself in their shoes. Empathy will take you a long way. As you are likely closer to the process which will produce the information, you may have a much better idea of what they really need. How do you think you will be viewed by management when you show initiative and prove that you can make life simpler not only for yourself, but for them as well? You can achieve this by thinking ahead and putting yourself in the senior management's shoes.

If you are having deeper issues with a request, and struggling to build an open dialogue with your manager, you should consider speaking with another manager who is on the same job grading. Approach them in confidence and ask for their view and advice.

These options have worked well for me in the past, so consider all your options. Always act on logic and never emotion when dealing with difficult circumstances. Out of all the above options, I would recommend talking with your management and pro-actively going and implementing positive change in your reporting. This is a very strong signal to management that you can lead change. It will help you build both confidence and credibility.

Define Success, Set Goals

We all have our dreams. Success to me may not mean the same thing as it does to you. Before you continue reading, write down what you feel life success means to you…

Now, take a moment to think about what you have written. Are the actions you are taking in your life helping you towards achieving your own success? Would you describe yourself as successful now? If not, why?

Asking yourself if you are on the right path to achieving your personal definition of success will keep your mindset aligned with your personal goals.

Now apply this thinking to your own role. What does success in your current role mean to you? Would you describe yourself as successful now? If not, why? Once you have defined what success in your job means to you, write down goals and timescales which will help you in achieving this. However, the point is to question yourself, "am I achieving the success I defined for this role?"

Manage Email

I have a love/hate relationship with my email. I love using email because it is easy to transfer information from me to my customer. But I also hate email because it is abused in organisations. Being copied in on totally irrelevant parts of someone's job is hugely frustrating. So how does one manage email to avoid frustration and time wasting? Think of email as being like your task list. If you leave thousands of emails just piling up in your inbox, it is easy to:

- Forget about your customer
- Become cluttered in your thinking
- Feel overworked
- Manage and prioritise tasks poorly

My advice on this topic is simple. First clear you inbox completely. When you receive your next email and you need to perform some kind of action, either deal with it now and archive/delete the email or leave it in your inbox until you can deal with it. At any given day I will have only between 7-10 emails in my inbox (and I receive hundreds of emails each day). These will represent tasks which I have been given and not yet completed or transferred. Leaving on time is a goal post, and so is the amount of emails which sit in your inbox at any given time.

If you set your mind to having a clear inbox, you will be focussed on removing waste on your daily task list. Finally, write down your task list every day at the very end of your working day. This is when activities are still fresh in your mind. This technique will help improve your task turn around and your reliability in remembering to serve your customer well.

Final Word on Mindset

"The mind is a powerful thing. It can take you through walls."

~ Denis Avey, The Man Who Broke Into Auschwitz: A True Story of World War II

If you cannot achieve something in your mind, how will you achieve it in reality? Take another moment to consider achieving your success in your own mind and now you will realise that it is you who sets your limits, not your company and not your management.

PART III: Automation: Financial Modelling Made Useful

☐

7 - Automation: Data Becomes Information

"The first rule of any technology used in a business is that automation applied to an efficient operation will magnify the efficiency. The second is that automation applied to an inefficient operation will magnify the inefficiency."

~ Bill Gates

In the introduction of this book, I told you about a true story in which I had once worked long hours, focussing more on using 'blood and sweat' rather than concentrating on improving processes. What changed the course of my life and career, started with the simple (yet difficult) decision to only work to 5:00 pm. However, the story does not end there. Simply leaving on time was not going to solve the issue. If, at the very minimum, I didn't achieve the same level of results by leaving on time, I would be sure to lose my job. The decision to leave earlier every day and achieve results was a daunting target to meet. But no risk, no champagne.

Three months after making the choice I was promoted, and the results were triple what anyone could have foreseen. The risk had paid off. But why? What was the driving force behind obtaining better results and accuracy? Other than focussing on processes, the simple answer was automation.

Automation was adopted in the following ways:

1)   Changing the way data was organised

2)   Having data readily available in the required format and having a system present it in a standardised way

To demonstrate a practical example of how this was used, we will take a specific task which was automated, "account reconciliations" *(1)*. For those of you who do not work in finance or understand what this means, account reconciliations put simply reflects information which makes up a specific recorded number in a system. For example, if you have an opening bank balance in January of £1000 and at the end of February show £700, this means your bank account balance had reduced £300. The reconciliation of what transpired to reduce your balance £300 is the equivalent of your bank statement. In accounting, there are many such accounts which require an explanation of what transpired between the opening balance and closing balance. Just like the bank statement example.

At the time of my story, management accountants were spending two days (at least) analysing and documenting what transactions had occurred during the month, and therefore what a closing account balance (at any given time) represented. This was due to an immense amount of transactional (data) recording, known as posting journals.

The first step was to organise the data! If one could record the data in a given way, it could be streamlined to fit the required 'account reconciliation format'. For one whole month any transaction which needed entering was done in a specific way which would enable automation of reporting later on. Each transaction had a text field assigned to it which provided a pre-defined description of the reason for this particular posting. By becoming vigilant about how data was being recorded, and setting up a pre-defined structure, I now had a way to load transactional data (journals) into a system which had qualitative information.

Now all that needed doing was automating a way to summarise the pre-defined categories of data into the required report summary format. That was it. I spent one hour each morning and evening for an entire month learning the very basics of VBA whilst travelling on the train. It was then time to practise my new found ability on programming Microsoft Excel to allocate the data (which had now been structured) into the required format.

This took about fifteen hours of learning, preparation and testing before the next deadline. I remember my colleagues wondering why I was creating my own workload; they could not understand why I was putting such a burden on myself. No one could have guessed. But the following month-end it came to the time for preparing account reconciliations again. The office groaned at the thought of preparing the arduous reports. Nobody enjoyed summarising hundreds of lines of data and summarising it into a story for some report which was never truly correct due to the volume of manual work. It was a painful task. However, this particular month-end was to be different…

After retrieving the 4000 lines of transactional data, I clicked the button "Run Account Reconciliations" in Microsoft Excel. In 2.5 minutes, the report had done the following:

1) Organised all data into their respective account categories

2) Explained (as per the new text field) why there was a change for a given posting

3) Summarised this information into a few lines (rather than lots of meaningless lines of transactional data)

4) Highlighted any errors which I could have made in my journal postings

Once this had run I spent a further twenty minutes checking the information. Not only had my accounting become more accurate, but so had my reporting. Most of the twenty minutes was spent making the report look clean and credible. This new process had saved me two days of work!

The kicker is that the information (being automated) was more traceable and accurate. Therefore the understanding of movements and business transactions occurring became more self-evident. Finally, automation had granted me two days to work on improving other processes. I was hooked! Within another month I had completed three more time saving projects, and the snowball effect became very evident when I had the time to train and help others. See the figure below for a summary of how the new process would work in the relevant stages.

Figure 7a – Account Reconciliation Automation Flow

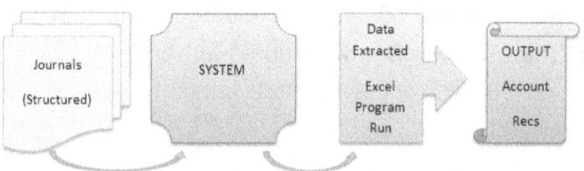

Data Structure

Without further delay, let us delve into the detail which will highlight how to make data very useful for you, by looking at data structure.

Data Positioning: In my opinion, it is always better to have data retrieved or pasted into one location when using a report. In other words if you have a report with many different requirements, rather than run several reports to fit each requirement, it is better to have one large report with more lines of transactional data.

For example, if you want to report sales by customer as well as by product separately, do not retrieve two sets of data tables to do this (one for customer and one for product). Rather, it may be more beneficial to make one report which includes both who the customer was, and which product code they purchased. Therefore, if one customer purchased 5 products you would have 5 rows of data rather than just one (for that customer). Your data table might look something like this:

Figure 7b – Data by Product

Customer	Product	Product Code	Year	Month	Currency	Sales Person	Amount
Pudding&Pie	Shape Shifter	4090	2013	1 GBP		Dave Ricks	200
Pudding&Pie	Ramp Analyser	1212	2013	3 GBP		Dave Ricks	100
Pudding&Pie	Book Wormer	2221	2013	4 GBP		Dave Ricks	100
Pudding&Pie	Jump Jacket	6781	2013	2 GBP		Sam Peters	200
Pudding&Pie	Stump Bumper	2872	2013	2 GBP		Joe McArthur	210
JozZola	Book Wormer	2221	2013	1 GBP		Sam Peters	400
JozZola	Jump Jacket	6781	2013	1 GBP		Joe McArthur	200

So what is the benefit of having a larger data report? The simple answer is the data report is not larger. It had just been consolidated into one place showing more transactions per customer sale. This means that you now only need to have one report run in order to report sales by customer and sales by product code. This also means that the data will tie up, because it is from the same report.

If someone was to ask, "Why have we only sold £500 to CocZola?" you would now have the ability to filter just this customer, and you would have the detail of what products were sold. Or you could have a report (PivotTable) do this for you on command. So positioning your data constructively in one place is very important.

Amount Column: Have amounts recorded in one column if possible. The reason for this will be evident in the following chapters. However, to illustrate the point imagine that you had lines of data with the amounts of sales under month columns rather than month rows. This would mean that your summary reporting would have 12 (Jan – Dec) columns to reference to get an amount instead of just one. In 'Figure 7b' above, you can see that there is just one column for Amount. This means that the amount column can be referenced easily using Lookups or SUMIF or PivotTable functions which we will move onto shortly.

Let us assume that you are often sent ad-hoc tasks which require you to complete templates using the same underlying data or information, but in different formats. If your data is structured like our example, it can be referenced using SUMIF formulas easily no matter what the format requirement. This will ensure that your reports are always completed in a consistent and accurate manner without much manual work. This will in fact help you to semi-automate your reporting, without even needing programming know-how.

To summarise, keep your data in one place (if possible) within any given report. Do not be afraid to ensure data is organised only by sets of rows with field headings such as the previous illustration. Even though this may make your data seem lengthy, it will be easy to reference later on and save you time on many types of requests.

☐

8 - Toolbox: Spreadsheet Functions and Techniques

"People of genius do not excel in any profession because they work in it, they work in it because they excel."

~ William Hazlitt

For this chapter I would recommend opening Microsoft Excel so you can try these techniques yourself. Many of you will already be well aware of the SUM function as well as many others. However, we are coming to some important techniques shortly, so stay with me on this one regardless of whether or not you are already experienced.

To be clear, this chapter is not due to any affiliation with Microsoft, but rather because Excel is the software with which I am most familiar and experienced. You can also download a free trial of Excel and other such applications on the internet if you have not already done so.

From reading Part I of this book you will already be familiar with what functions (or formulas) are, and be ready to start trying these out for yourself. But before we move on to any 'tricks of the trade' let us become familiar with the basics.

As you will know by now, Excel is made up of rows (shown by numbers on a vertical axis) and columns (shown by letters on a horizontal axis).

The white blocks with greyish borders will be referred to as Cell Ranges, or 'Cells'. For example, if I refer to Cell 'AD3', which I will show as '$AD$3' (putting dollar signs to separate rows from columns in my description), this will relate to the Cell reference below which is highlighted:

Figure 8a – Cell Reference $AD$3

You can type anything you like into the 'Cells', whether it be text, numbers, or even dates.

Functions – SUM

Let us start with something simple, like a simple SUM formula.

In Cells A1:A6, type the following names/text and Cells B1:B5 the following amounts/numbers:

	A	B	C
1	John	10	
2	Sandy	10	
3	Fred	20	
4	Jessica	25	
5	Ned	30	
6	TOTAL		

You will notice that we left out a total for all the amounts. This is where our function will come in, the SUM function.

In Cell B6 type,

=SUM(B1:B5)

Tip: Instead of typing in the Cell reference, after entering in the open bracket, "(", you can highlight the Cells you wish to highlight. Then type, ")".

You will now see something which looks like this:

Figure 8b, SUM function example

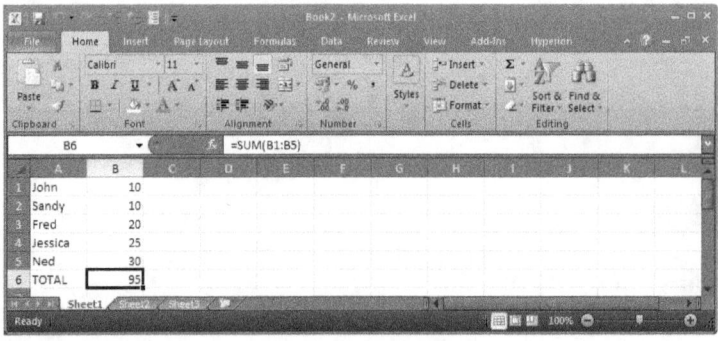

The difference between a formula and a function is that a formula may contain a function. For example, you could have the following entered into a Cell reference:

= SUM(B1:B5) + 10 /2

This will give you the answer 100 as you have the SUM calculating 95, but then you are adding 10/2, which equals 5.

95 + 5 = 100.

Functions – SUMIF Technique

Type the following information into a new spreadsheet:

This is representative of transactional data. It represents product sales made to specific customers. In your day-to-day job you may be sent information which you have to manually add up, or have to analyse. In this scenario we are going to summarise all the "Rangatang" products sold.

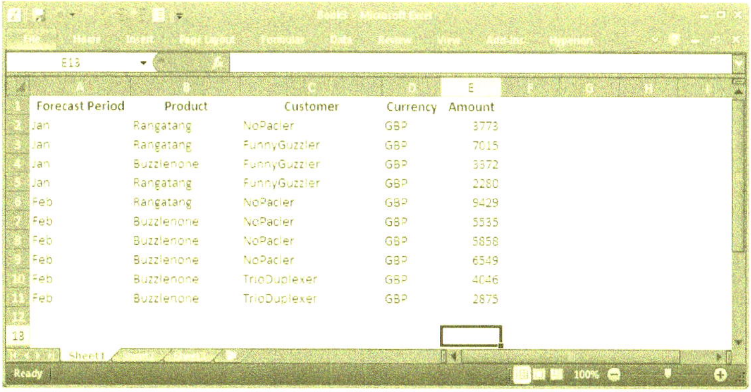

In Cell $E$13 type the following,

=SUMIF($B$2:$B$11,"Rangatang",$E$2:$E$11)

You will notice as you typed that the following syntax support appears:

Figure 8d. Syntax Support

Once you type the open brackets Excel helps you to identify the various parts of the function. The first part is called the "range". In a SUMIF, the range represents what items you want the application to look at and SUM given a specific "criteria".

Therefore, after you type in a comma, the very next item you told the application you want to reference was the product, "Rangatang." Finally, after typing another comma, you now want Excel to return only the amounts relating to your product, Rangatang.

After you type the return (Enter) key, you should have an amount which shows as £22,497.
Much easier than adding this up yourself, right?!

Figure 8e, New SUMIF

	Forecast Period	Product	Customer	Currency	Amount
1	Forecast Period	Product	Customer	Currency	Amount
2	Jan	Rangatang	NoPacler	GBP	3773
3	Jan	Rangatang	FunnyGuzzler	GBP	7015
4	Jan	Buzzlenone	FunnyGuzzler	GBP	3372
5	Jan	Rangatang	FunnyGuzzler	GBP	2280
6	Feb	Rangatang	NoPacler	GBP	9429
7	Feb	Buzzlenone	NoPacler	GBP	5535
8	Feb	Buzzlenone	NoPacler	GBP	5858
9	Feb	Buzzlenone	NoPacler	GBP	6549
10	Feb	Buzzlenone	TrioDuplexer	GBP	4046
11	Feb	Buzzlenone	TrioDuplexer	GBP	2875
12					
13					22497

Note: We used the "$" in our function. This instructs Excel to fix a specified set of rows or columns to a specific place. Therefore if you were to copy the formula to other Cells, Excel would remember to still look at those particular rows or columns and not reference an incorrect location.

Now to show you the 'trick of the trade'! Imagine that you have thousands of lines of data and you wish to build a report that SUMS only Rangatang products as well as only referencing the FunnyGuzzler customer. How would you do this? Concatenation! In other words, join the two together. The best way to demonstrate is to illustrate. Type the following into Cell $F$2:

=B2&C2

You should return something which looks like, "RangatangNoPacler". You will also notice, that this time, we did not use the "$" sign in our Cell referencing. The reason is because we are going to copy the formulas down all rows which contain data. The quickest way to do this (other than copy and paste) is to double click on the fill handle of the Cell you have just changed. This looks like a small black box on the bottom right hand corner of the Cell which you have highlighted. Your data should now look like the below:

Figure 8f, Concatenation and Fill Handle

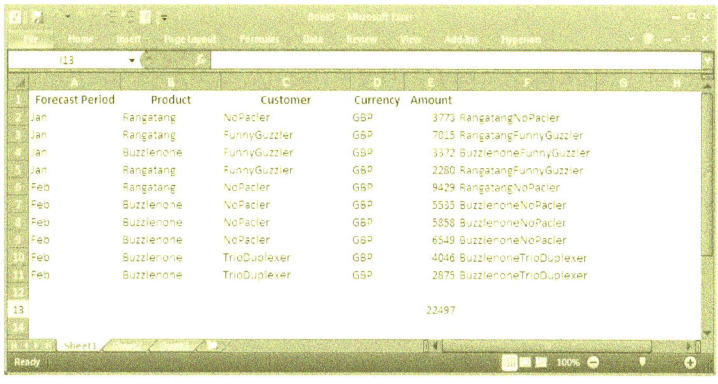

Now in Cell $E$14, type the following:

=SUMIF($F$2:$F$11,"RangatangFunnyGuzzler",$E$2:$E$11)

If you have done all of the above correctly and returned a value of £9,295, well done! You will have a dataset which looks like this:

Figure 8g, End Result

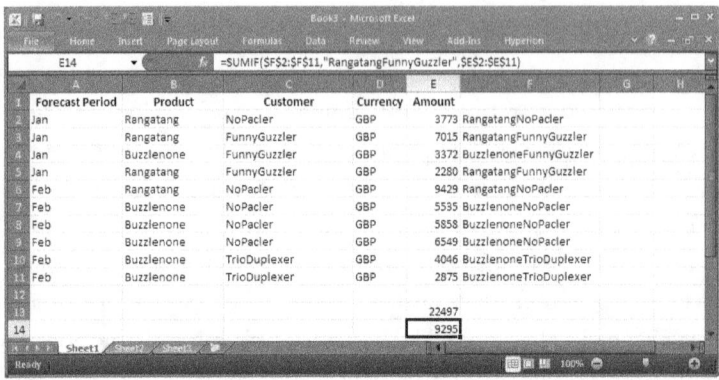

Another way of achieving the result would be to use a SUMIFS function instead of concatenation. However, this is enough for the time being. I prefer to use the above method because it will be easier for others to follow and for you to manipulate later on if required.

I must highlight that this can be an extremely powerful method when used correctly. If you want to get more advanced, try the following:

1. On Sheet2, type "Jan" in Cell $B$3 and "Feb" in Cell $C$3, "Jan" again in $E$3 and "Feb" again in $F$3

2. Then type Rangatang in $A$4

3. In Cells $B$2 and $C$2, type FunnyGuzzler

4. Then in $E$2 and $F$2 type NoPacler. Resize all columns if you wish and to your liking

5.   Go to Sheet1. On Cell $F$2 type, "=B2&C2&A2". Then double click the Fill Handle again so that this copies down as before

6.   Go to Sheet2 and in Cell $B$4 type,

=SUMIF(Sheet1!$F$2:$F$11,Sheet2!$A4&Sheet2!B$2&Sheet2!B$3,Sheet1!$E$2:$E$11)

7.   After returning a value of £9,295, copy this (highlight and press CNTRL + C), then paste (CNTRL + V) in Cells $C$4, $E$4 and $F$4.

If you have done all of the above correctly, you should have something that looks like this:

Figure 8h. Summary Report I

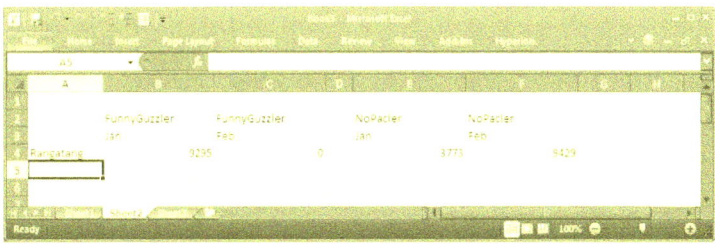

If you have gotten this far, then EXCELLENT! Here is your prize, overtype Cell $A$4 with "Buzzlenone". You should see something like this:

Figure 8i, Summary Report II

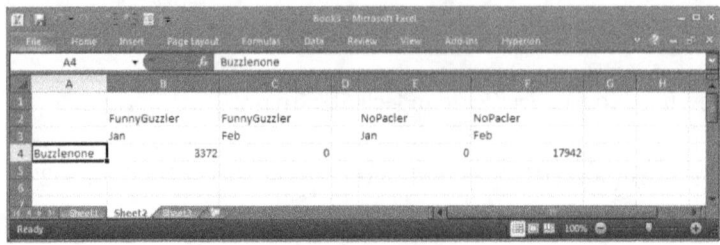

Fantastic! You have just grasped the concept that you can create a dynamic summary report. Whenever you change an input, in this case the Product description, numbers which may be useful to your decision making will literally appear. Go ahead and mess around with this by changing different headings etc. to match the data options you have.

Do you know how this just worked? Well, let's take another look at your function:

=SUMIF(Sheet1!$F$2:$F$11,Sheet2!$A4&Sheet2!B$2&Sheet2!B$3,Sheet1!$E$2:$E$11)

You will note first the "Sheet1" reference. This is because you are currently on the report summary, Sheet2. Therefore, the function needed to know you were locating Sheet1. Then, between the first and second comma you will need to note the following text:

"Sheet2!$A4&Sheet2!B$2&Sheet2!B$3"

Ignore the Sheet2 reference and it will look something like this

"A4&B$2&B$3"

Well this is matching the text, "BuzzlenoneFunnyGuzzlerJan". Therefore Excel is determining this as the Criteria. It is referencing all Cells on Sheet1 that you highlighted in Cells "$F$2:$F$11" and summing them only if they match "BuzzlenoneFunnyGuzzlerJan".

Congratulations on creating a dynamic report from scratch. Take a break, and give yourself a pat on the back… now let us move on! You will need to save this workbook in order to progress to the next part.

PivotTable, a SUMIF Replication

Let us assume that the earlier SUMIF example was more of an "ad-hoc" analysis than something you will be doing on a regular basis. You may want to analyse data and filter only by information which you care about at the present time. To start with you are going to replicate the exact same summary, except this time using a PivotTable.

1) First, go to Sheet1 where your data is

2) Drag your curser over Cells "$A$1:$E$11" by holding down the left click button on your mouse. You should have a page which looks like the following:

Figure Pivot I: Highlighting Data

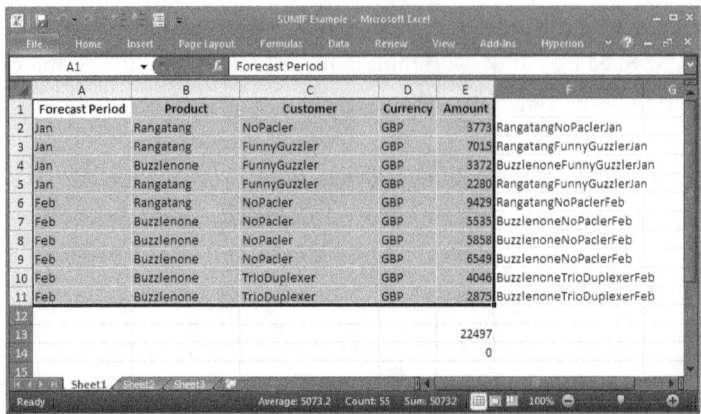

3) Now click on the "Insert" Ribbon at the top of your Excel window and select PivotTable. The following window will appear:

Figure Pivot II: Setting Up PivotTable

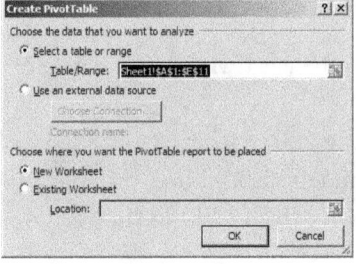

Just click "Ok" and this will create a new sheet for you in which you will construct your PivotTable.

WARNING: If you did not highlight the correct columns or one of your columns excluded a heading then Excel will not allow you to run the PivotTable.

You will now have a screen which looks like the image below:

Figure Pivot III: A Blank Canvas

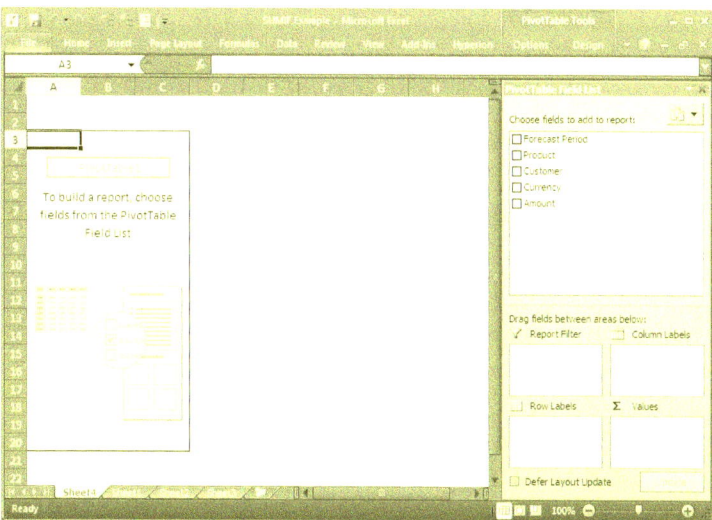

Take special notice of the "PivotTable Field List" on the right hand side of the screen. The application has identified your data headings. You will now be allowed to drag these into rows or columns which suit your reporting requirements. In this case we want a report which will provide the same format as the SUMIF example.

If you recall the previous summary on Sheet2, the columns consisted first of **'Customer'** information, then **'Forecast Period'** and finally a row showing the **'Product'** information. In your PivotTable you will treat this exactly the same way. Look at the four boxes to the bottom right of the image. These consist of a Report Filter, Column Labels, Row Labels and Values. The first item we will prepare is the Column Labels area.

1) Hold your curse over the **'Customer'** field and drag-and-drop this into the Column Labels section

2) Repeat Step1 for the **'Forecast Period'** and drag this underneath **'Customer'** in the Column Labels. The reason you are dragging this underneath, is because our previous summary had 'Forecast Period' as a column heading after 'Customer'.

3) Repeat the same process as Step1 again for **'Product'**. Except this time, drag into the Row Labels area.

4) Finally, you need some values so drag the **'Amount'** field into the Values area.

If you completed all the above steps correctly, you should end up with something which resembles the following:

Figure Pivot IV: Final PivotTable

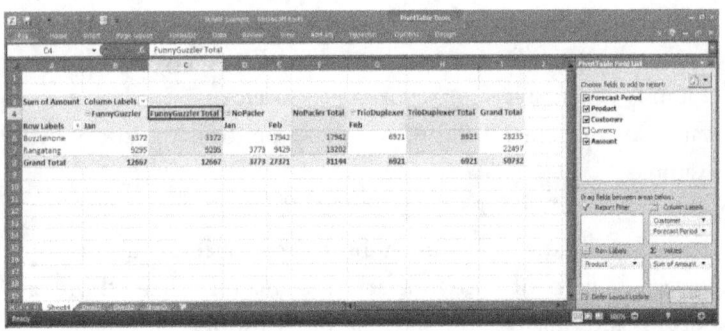

Great stuff! You now understand how a PivotTable works. You can also click on the drop down arrows as well as filter certain items which may be important to you. Also take special note of the Design ribbon located at the top of your window. This can help you format the PivotTable to look much more professional.

In the below image I have removed the 'Totals' (by selecting them and pressing "CNTRL + -" on my keyboard) and then performed some fancy work using the Design ribbon. Finally, I switched 'Product' and 'Customer' to show in the Row Labels and 'Forecast Period' to remain as a Column Label. See if you can replicate something to look like this:

Figure Pivot V : Final PivotTable Revised

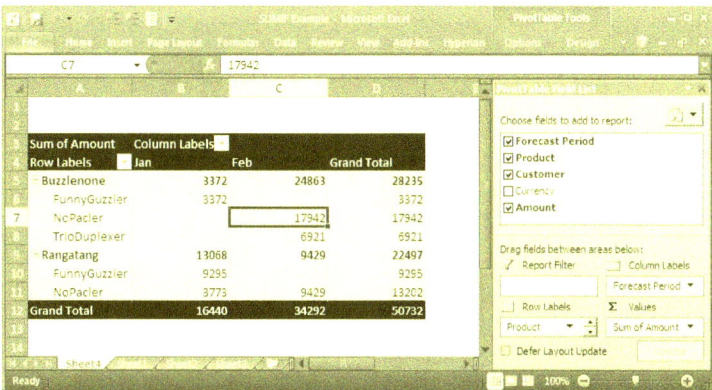

One note regarding PivotTables; when new data is added these can expand or contract in size. If I am building and standardising a model typically I will revert to using a SUMIF approach as the report can usually be kept to a specified size, and if new fields are added I will need to consider whether or not these should be taken into account.

Enjoy this tool like the others, it is very powerful. In the past I have used this approach to allow sales teams to see what profits and revenues were generated from their sales. They were then able to drill into customer and product information without the need for wasting time constructing the information themselves, or emailing me with questions. A one-stop-shop for sales information which rendered many other reporting tasks obsolete, thereby saving the sales organisation and me time!

Functions – VLOOKUP on the Stock Market

In this section we are going to take open-source stock market information and create a reference to tell us what the open and closing price was for the Yahoo stock on a given day within 2011.

First you will need to locate some data. We will analyse the open-source data by going to:

http://uk.finance.yahoo.com/q/hp?s=YHOO&b=01&a=00&c =2011&e=31&d=11&f=2011&g=d

Now click on "Download to Spreadsheet" as shown below:

Figure 8j, Extracting Yahoo Stock Prices into Excel from the Internet

This should then appear in Excel within a sheet called "table". You may have to open the file first, depending on whether you saved the data or not.

Figure 8k, Yahoo Stock Prices In Excel

![Excel spreadsheet showing Yahoo stock prices table]

Now insert a new sheet by clicking the following symbol:

Figure 8l, Insert New Sheet

On the new sheet in Cell $C$4 and $D$4, type the reference "Open" and "Close" respectively.

In Cell $A$5 type in the reference 01/06/2011. For this example, we will use European date format whereby month will be after the first "/".

So far nothing fantastic, right? What we are hoping for is that some magic will happen whenever we enter a date. Specifically, we want a magic Function to return the open price (and another for the close price) of the Yahoo stock for the 01/06/2011.

First, you need to become familiar with which function to use, in this case the "VLOOKUP". This function will examine a set of rows which you designate. When it finds the criteria that you specify, it will return a value in a column you specify. We want a function which will look at all the dates, then, when it finds the date we want, it must return a value of the Yahoo stock Open price. We will then build a separate formula to analyse the close price using a different column reference.

Without further ado type in the following on Sheet1 Cell reference $C$5,

=VLOOKUP(

The Syntax will show (**lookup_value**, **table_array**, **col_index_num**, **[range_lookup]**).

lookup_value: This relates to the value you wish to look up. In this case we wish to lookup the date. Therefore type in "$A$5," to represent the date which needs to be referenced.

table_array: This relates to the area or "array" you want the function to examine. For the purpose of this illustration we will use all the stock market data. Here you will then want to highlight all the data or type,

table!$A$1:$G$253,

col_index_num: Now that you have the column "A" all the way to column "G" highlighted, you need to know which column to reference. In this case we want to reference the Yahoo "Open" price. The open prices are in column "B". Column "B" is one column away from the starting reference, column "A". Therefore, the column number is 2. So in your function type,

2,

range_lookup: This is not mandatory because it is bracketed in "[ ]" brackets. However, it is advisable. Let me explain why. If 01/06/2011 does not appear in the data, the VLOOKUP might find the nearest match possible. We want the VLOOKUP to return a value only if there is a 01/06/2011 in the data. So here we will type,

FALSE)

Finally, you should have entered into Cell $C$5 a Function which looks like the following,

=VLOOKUP($A5,table!$A$1:$G$253,2,FALSE)

If you have done this correctly, you will see the value 16.34. Well done! Just copy this formula and paste it into Cell $D$5. Except now you will need to change the column reference to show the "Close" price. This is the fifth column from the reference point so make sure that you change the **col_index_num** from "2" to "5".

You should have a value returned of 15.85.

Excellent! Your model will look like this:

Figure 8m, Insert New Sheet

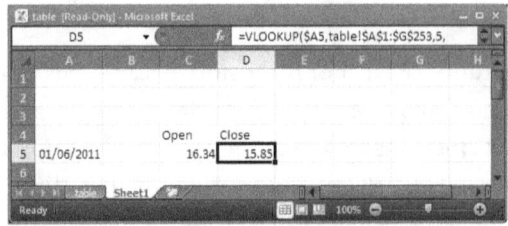

Now save your workbook as you will need this again soon. The good news is that whenever you overwrite the date in Cell $A$5, the corresponding Open and Close stock price of the Yahoo stock will automaticaly appear. Magic? Hardly, just some basic yet extremely effective spreadsheet know-how.

Functions – IF You Could IF

IF. One of the most useful techniques you can learn when building models, analysing data or having automated control checks, is the IF Function. Think about this logically, we are always using the word "if" in our thinking. Some examples may look like this,

"If the ROI (Return On Investment) is below 10%, then reject this project. Otherwise, accept this project."

"If the sales person's score is above 10, then mark the sales person as a '5-star seller'. Otherwise, mark them as below 5-star."

"If the total in my report does not tie to the total sum of my data, there must be an error. Otherwise, everything is fine."

Earlier on we discussed how almost any process which requires logic can be automated. You only need to look at the above examples to realise that all of these require pure logic, "If this, then do that".

For illustration purposes we are going to continue with the report you designed in the previous "VLOOKUP on Stock Market" Function walkthrough. So go ahead and open this if you have not already done so.

Objective: Create a formula which flags "Up" if the Yahoo stock price closed above its open on a given day or "Down" if the Yahoo stock price closed below its open on a given day.

Solution: In Cell $F$5 on Sheet1, add in the following formula,

   =$D$5-$C$5

In other words subtract the Open price from the Close price. If the figure returned is negative, this means that the stock closed lower than its Open price and visa-versa. We want to add an IF Function which will tell us in plain English whether the stock went "Up" or "Down". In Cell $G$5, type the following

   =IF(

You will note the following automatically appears in the Syntax:

logical_test: In the logic sentence we had earlier as,

"If the ROI (Return On Investment) is below 10%, then reject this project. Otherwise, accept this project."

The "If the ROI is below 10%" part of this sentence relates to the logical_test. Whatever value we returned earlier in Cell $F$5 will be part of our current logic test. Our logic test is that "IF" the $F$5 value is less or more than zero. We will use less than, but not for any particular reason, just as an example.

To further construct your function type,

=IF($F$5<0,

You have now completed the first and most complicated part.

[value_if_true]: This is more self-explanatory. What do you want to happen if the value is less than zero (in other words TRUE to the **logical_test**). In our objective, we specified that there must be a returned text of "Down". So in this case, type the following,

=IF($F$5<0, **"Down",**

You have now stipulated that if the first logic part of your Function becomes true, then the returned value must be "Down".

[value_if_false]: Let is continue from the **value_if_true** example. Let us say that the **logical_test** or first part of the function would return a value above zero. This would render the **value_if_true** useless, because it simply is not TRUE. It is not less than zero. Therefore, it is FALSE. So now you need to complete your Function by typing,

=IF($F$5<0,"Down",**"Up")**

Well done! If you have completed this correctly, you will note that the stock price reduced on the 01/06/2011 and thus the IF Function has returned "Down". A lot of this may seem quite technical, but how would you think about it in your mind? You would think, "Yahoo's stock price closed lower on the 01/06/2011, so it went down". Logical is it not?

Figure 8n, IF Statement

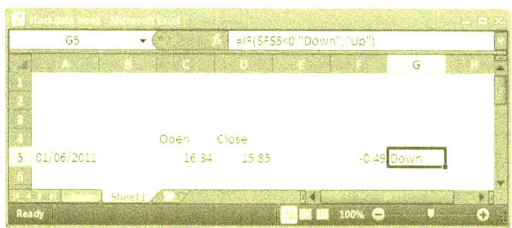

The point is that you could put many different formulas in the, say, value_if_false section. It did not have to be the example I have chosen. I recommend that you test this out and try to be creative in your approach to working with formulas. You can use IF statements in many different ways and if your job entails checking numbers, text or even dates, this can be a powerful weapon to add to your arsenal of continuous improvement ideas.

A Note on Putting Functions and Formulas Together

There is a difference between Functions and Formulas. Remember - Formulas can contain Functions. Try combining IF, VLOOKUP and SUM formulas inside one another. For example, you can have a formula such as,

=IF(VLOOKUP(SUM()),SUMIF(),"No"))

Be creative with your approach to formula writing. Use the logic in your own mind to help drive a formula which you may wish to create. More than anything try to automate a system to work for you. Learn the skills you need to improve; but start with believing that it is possible.

A Note on Presentation

The presentation in the previous examples leaves much which can be improved on. Experiment with different fonts, colours, shading, borders and sizing of cells. I often try to fit colour schemes in line with the organisations logo. Get creative here. Leave a stamp. When others review your work and can see you have taken pride in presentation, this can lead to the belief that you have taken pride in the accuracy and quality of your work too.

It takes five minutes to improve the look of even the most ad-hoc report. It is worth doing. The customer pays for quality so give it to them!

9 - Creativity Evokes Change

"If you hear a voice within you say, 'You cannot paint,' then by all means paint, and that voice will be silenced".

~ Vincent Van Gogh

The wonderful vibration of sound would run through the ground where I would sit with my head resting against the piano. I was eight years old and music had become a huge part of my being. I never achieved 'grades' when learning the piano, because they didn't interest me. The thing I always loved the most about music was to create it.

Creativity

Creativity is what has set man apart from the apes. To start something from nothing can be a hugely rewarding experience. A guitar is just a set of strings on a wooden box with a hole in the middle. However, the sweet sound it makes depending on what you create with it, can change your mood for an entire day. To me, creating music is about grasping the basics and then making something magnificent happen by improvising! As I have said before, you do not need to be highly advanced to be highly efficient. You just need to know the basics and make something happen from there on. Build upon progress, and before you know it you will have achieved a master piece.

Creativity in the office is of the utmost importance. We need to be creative in order to solve problems as well as achieve personal satisfaction. Why is this so important? Because if you are stressed and burnt out, you are unlikely to be productive. On the other hand, if you have energy and motivation, you are likely to be. And if you have clarity of thought, you will tackle decisions far more efficiently. You need to make time for yourself so that you can use the energy you need to be productive. If you are productive, you will free up more time in your day to drive further productivity. More time in your day means more choice in the additional hours you want to work (if any) and whether you are suffering from stress or reaping moments of restfulness and joy.

The point is to be creative in your approach to problem solving. When using financial modelling, take the basic building blocks in this book and develop them into something more. Always build on your knowledge and experience.

Final Word

Remember that Lean is not about you. Yet it does require you to take action. One way of getting started is to identify your key restraints and ask for help in creative problem solving by forming a team. Once you have 'cleaned up your own sandbox,' you can go and play in somebody else's. Push yourself to help others. Push yourself to extend beyond your limits because your limits will then be extended. Believe that you are capable of achieving great things, which may seem far out of your reach today.

I have always been a believer in the 'aim small, miss small' approach. Often we decide our own limits. This starts with your mindset. Set your mind and beliefs to greater limits and you will reach higher highs. The opposite is also true. Your mind is a powerful weapon when equipped with courage and belief in one's own ability.

Most of all have a mind to improve your surroundings and evoke positive change. Remain strong and open minded when receiving criticism but keep focussed on defining your success and reaching your goals.

Thank you.

Dedicated to my wife, *Suzanne*

GLOSSARY

1) Account Reconciliation: "In accounting, reconciliation refers to a process that compares two sets of records (usually the balances of two accounts) to make sure they are in agreement. Reconciliation is used to ensure that the money leaving an account matches the actual money spent, this is done by making sure the balances match at the end of a particular accounting period." – taken from http://en.wikipedia.org/wiki/Reconciliation_(accounting)

2) Analysis: A process of breaking down information whereby one can make a decision to derive corrective action in management control and leadership.

3) Bottleneck: Whereby the performance or capacity of a process is limited by a stoppage or problem-activity.

4) Flow: Used to describe the way tasks or activities connect seamlessly or efficiently in an overall process.

5) JIT (Just in Time): Philosophy used in manufacturing to describe purchasing and using material as you require it, avoiding holding and managing costs.

6) Kaizen: Japanese for 'continuous improvement'. Whereby, one should take the philosophy to seek process perfection.

7) Kanban: Japanese for 'signboard' or used to represent a signal, usually one which is visible. An example would be traffic lights which could be seen as Kanban, red meaning stop and green meaning go.

8) KPI (Key Performance Indicator): Calculations or information which serves as an indication of performance related to a respective subject.

9) Lean: Management philosophy derived from the Toyota Production System. The Lean philosophy seeks to create value and eliminate waste by focusing on process flow.

10) Process: In business this relates to activities or tasks that lead to the production of a product or service, usually for a customer.

11) Red Tagging: A process used to mark all visible items within a workshop area. When each item is used over 30 days, the mark (or Red Tag) is removed. The items left with markers are considered less important or waste as they are not used frequently.

12) TAKT Time: A calculation which sets a target in value stream process mapping in which activities must fall within.

13) Troubleshoot: An activity of trial and error in problem-solving.

14) Throughput: The movements of inputs and outputs through a production process.

15) Value Stream Mapping: An exercise of breaking down a process into its constituent parts and tasks and mapping how these are performed.

16) 5S: Sort, Set-in-Order, Shine, Standardise and Sustain. This is one of the underlying techniques of Lean implementation discussed in Chapter 4.

BIBLIOGRAPHY

Print Books

Dweck, Carol. Mindset: The New Psychology of Success, Ballantine Books; Reprint edition, December 2007. Print

For Dummies (Harvey, Greg). Excel 2010 All-in-One For Dummies, For Dummies; 1 edition, May 2010. Print

For Dummies (Walkenbach, John). Excel VBA Programming For Dumnmies, For Dummies; 3 edition, February 2013. Print

Gray, John. MEN ARE FROM MARS, Women Are from Venus, Harper Paperbacks; Reprint edition, April 2012. Print.

Harris, Chris. Lean Connections: Making Information Flow Efficiently and Effectively, Productivity Press; 1 edition, June 2008. Print.

Kiyosaki, Robert T. Rich Dad Poor Dad: What The Rich Teach Their Kids About Money That the Poor and Middle Class Do Not!. Plata Publishing, August 2011. Print.

Womack, James P. Lean Thinking: Banish Waste and Create Wealth in Your Corporation, Revised and Updated. Productivity Press; 2nd edition, June 2003. Print.

Websites

cardiff.ac.uk (date not published). The Five Principles of Lean Thinking, Retrieved 18 May 2013 from http://www.cardiff.ac.uk/lean/principles/

forbes.com (9 Dec 2012). 8 Wastes of Lean, Retrieved 18 May 2013
from http://www.isixsigma.com/dictionary/8-wastes-of-lean/

isixsigma.com (13 May 2013). Why Working More than 8 Hours A
Day Can Kill You, Retrieved 18 May 2013 from
http://www.forbes.com/sites/daviddisalvo/2012/09/12/why-
working-more-than-8-hours-a-day-can-kill-you/

leansecrets.co.uk (4 Jan 2012). Lean Quotes, Retrieved 18 May 2013
from http://leansecrets.co.uk/tag/lean-quotes/

operational-excellence-consulting.com (date not published). 5S Visual
Workplace, Retrieved 18 May 2013 from http://www.operational-
excellence-consulting.com/our-opex-solutions/5s-visual-
workplace.html

theleanthinker.com (28 Apr 2010). THE LEAN THINKER, Retrieved
18 May 2013 from http://theleanthinker.com/2010/04/28/takt-time-
cycle-time/

wiki.answers.com (date not published). What is excel used for,
Retrieved 18 May 2013 from
http://wiki.answers.com/Q/What_is_excel_used_for

wikipedia.org (Jul 2008). Reconciliation (accounting), Retrieved 18 May
2013 from http://en.wikipedia.org/wiki/Reconciliation_(accounting)

wikipedia.org (last modified 14 May 2013). Value stream mapping,
Retrieved 18 May 2013 from
http://en.wikipedia.org/wiki/Value_stream_mapping

☐

☐

NOTES

www.ingramcontent.com/pod-product-compliance
Lightning Source LLC
Chambersburg PA
CBHW051328170526
45166CB00002B/731

* 9 7 8 1 4 8 9 5 6 0 8 9 6 *